Rewritten & Rising

A 90-Day Journey to Healing & Restoration after Betrayal, Abuse, and Brokenness in Marriage

Darah Ashlie

Copyright © 2025 by Darah Ashlie

All rights reserved.

The reflections and practices shared here are intended to support spiritual and emotional well-being. They are not meant to replace medical, psychological, or other professional advice. Please seek appropriate help from a licensed professional when needed.

No part of this publication may be reproduced, distributed, or transmitted in any form or by any means, including photocopying, recording, or other electronic or mechanical methods, without the prior written permission, except as permitted by U.S. copyright law. For permission requests, contact: www.darahashlie.com/contact

Unless otherwise noted, Scripture quotations are taken from The Holy Bible, New International Version®, NIV®. Copyright © 1973, 1978, 1984, 2011 by Biblica, Inc. Used with permission of Zondervan. All rights reserved worldwide. www.zondervan.com

Scriptures marked NKJV are from THE NEW KING JAMES VERSION. © 1982 by Thomas Nelson, Inc. Used by permission. All rights reserved.

Scriptures marked ESV are from THE ENGLISH STANDARD VERSION. © 2001 by Crossway Bibles, a division of Good News Publishers.

Scriptures marked NLT are from Holy Bible, New Living Translation. © 1996. Used by permission of Tyndale House Publishers, Inc., Wheaton, Illinois 60189. All rights reserved.

Scriptures marked MSG are from *The Message* by Eugene H. Peterson. © 1993, 1994, 1995, 1996, 2000. Used by permission of NavPress Publishing Group. All rights reserved.

For privacy reasons, names, locations, and dates may have been changed.

Book Cover: Kam Bains

Book Editor: Megan Tatreau

Interior Kingfisher Painting by Monica Avalos

First edition 2025

ISBN: 979-8-9938025-0-3

Ordering Information:

For bulk orders, special discounts are available for organizations, ministries, and other groups. For details visit www.darahashlie.com/contact and include "Bulk Inquiry" in the subject line.

*For every woman who has ever felt
broken, unseen, or unworthy—this is for you.
Your story is not over; it's being rewritten
so you can rise higher.*

*To my son—I'm so proud of the man you're becoming.
Your kindness and enthusiasm for life are contagious. Watching
you carry your light into the world has been my greatest joy.*

Contents

From My Heart to Yours _____ 5

Foundations For Your Journey _____ 8

Restoring Safety _____ 20

Devotionals Day 1-23 _____ 21

Investing in Stability _____ 92

Devotionals Day 24-53 _____ 93

Speaking Your Story _____ 187

Devotionals Day 54-72 _____ 188

Emerging Stronger _____ 246

Devotionals Day 73-90 _____ 247

Additional Resources: _____ 298

D.A.N.G.E.R. Check _____ 299

About the Author _____ 302

Notes _____ 303

From My Heart to Yours

If you're holding this book in your hands, you're doing a brave and difficult thing. You're probably experiencing very real, raw, and powerful emotions that led our paths to cross here. I truly understand how hard, even gut wrenching it can be to confront the issues in your marriage. This is a tender and sacred place to be.

This book is for women who find themselves confused, overwhelmed, and exhausted in their marriage. Women who are trying to discern what is happening. Women who find themselves in survival mode instead of leading a thriving and healthy life. If you look around and all you can see is the unkempt spaces in your life because it takes all you have to stay afloat while your marriage feels like it's sinking, then this book is for you.

For many years, I searched for what you're holding in your hands now. My own marriage was being dismantled, one painful memory after another. I tried for a time to unsee what I was seeing. I clung desperately to the belief that things weren't as bad as they were. I kept myself busy serving others and quietly set my soul wounds aside. But as my family moved from one mission field to the next, stateside and abroad, I felt myself slipping further and further away from who I once was.

Looking back, I believe there were things that could have helped me understand my situation sooner. I wrote this book as the resource I wished I had back then. I spent years praying, studying, writing to process my pain, and journaling my steps to healing. This book was born from those moments.

These pages are also shaped by years spent studying trauma and abuse, first in my own life, and then in the lives of the women I've been honored to walk alongside in my coaching practice. Like you, they have also traveled this winding road. This path to healing and hope is well-trodden.

I've shared pieces of my own story so that you know you're not alone here. I, too, am a survivor. The experiences I share are from relationships I've had since I was young—many shaped by trauma and abuse, and some by my own mistakes along the way. To protect the privacy of those involved, names have been left out. I have forgiven and truly moved on and can finally and honestly say I hope the same for those who have played a role in shaping who I am today—no matter what they may have done. I believe this has been a crucial part of my own healing.

I know the depth of pain caused by being in relationships where love, trust, and even faith should have been present, but instead, cycles of hurt and disappointment prevailed. Yet, even in those seasons, God met me with His grace, protection, and wisdom. I share these parts of my heart and story so you can see that healing is possible, and that God has a great hope for you, too—even in the moments when life feels overwhelming.

Other stories found in these pages reflect the lived experiences of women who have navigated abuse, confusion, and the journey toward healing. These stories are not based on any one person, but instead are composites that are used to represent common threads found in abuse and the common hope of coming out of it. While the names have been excluded and timelines changed, the heart of the stories—the struggles as well as the hope—are all real.

Now that you and I are a bit more acquainted, let me start our time together by giving you a glimpse of what you'll find here. What you're about to read is part guide and part devotional. In these pages you'll find grace for what feels like your messiness. You'll find empathy and compassion for your deepest wounds. And I hope you find a path toward freedom and healing.

Consider these pages a space for holding your pain and a path for moving out of it. Sometimes what you find here may feel raw, and at other times it may feel like experiencing freedom, like a winged bird finally discovering the key to escape the cage it once called home. Sit with both. Allow yourself the space and time to grieve what you've lost and the grace to notice and welcome even the smallest moments of joy as you move through this guide, perhaps for the first time in a very long time. Wherever the Holy Spirit leads you, allow Him to take you there.

At the heart of all that is written here is the heart of the Father. This is a guide for the woman seeking God's heart for her hurt and answers to the burning questions in her marriage. I hope it can serve as a safe haven for you. A place where you can reconnect with God's truths, rediscover your God-given identity, and experience the peace and clarity He longs to give you.

I also hope this book will help you find your footing as you take your next steps and begin to reclaim the voice others have tried to silence. I have been praying for you as you seek healing and hope in the hard and messy moments. Wherever you are on your journey, thank you for allowing me to walk alongside you.

Thinking of you,

Darah Ashlie

Foundations For Your Journey

I want to share a few things that I hope will support you as you move through this devotional. First, this book was written as a companion guide for a program I created called RISE, which helps women move from confusion to clarity in their marriages. Each devotional is designed to complement what you're learning in community, counseling, or a structured program, because while we're most often wounded in relationships, God can use safe, supportive connections to guide us toward healing.

As you begin to find clarity in your marriage and life, it's important to remember that healing is rarely done alone. I once heard it said that the extent to which we allow ourselves to be known is the extent to which we can be healed—and I believe there is truth to this. We all need spaces where we can be fully seen, understood, and supported. There is much to be learned from the experiences of others, so finding your tribe and surrounding yourself with a caring community can be profoundly nourishing.

Alongside your support system, this book is intended to accompany you on your healing journey, with devotionals that build from one day to the next, following the RISE model:

Restoring Safety
Investing in Stability & Self-care
Speaking Our Truth
Emerging Stronger

The RISE journey is based on a butterfly's transformation—a process of quiet, often unseen metamorphosis that mirrors the work God does in our hearts, minds, and bodies as we begin healing. As the caterpillar retreats into its cocoon, leaving the familiar behind, it enters a season of stillness and vulnerability where everything seems hidden and uncertain. But inside its cocoon, change is happening at a deep, cellular level. Wings are forming, strength is building, and a new life is quietly taking shape, even though the world outside sees nothing.

That little caterpillar is in a place of safety while it's being renewed and changed from the inside out so it can emerge transformed. In the same way, the RISE journey invites you to move through seasons of rest, stability, growth, and strength. Each phase builds on the last, helping you first to restore safety, invest in healing and stability, find your voice, and ultimately emerge from your struggles stronger and ready to spread your wings.

You may not see the transformation as it's happening, and some days may feel slow or impossible, but this time of quiet work is exactly what allows your strength to emerge. By the end of the journey, you are ready to unfold your wings, reclaim your story, and embrace the life God has been preparing for you all along. From the depths of darkness, God still has plans for you sweet friend.

While it may be tempting to skip ahead in what you're about to read, I want to encourage you to stay the course and read what you find each day as it comes, so we can walk this journey together—step by step. Once you've completed it, it works great as a daily devotional to return to on any given day.

However, not every woman will be in the same place on her journey. So, if you come across a devotional that doesn't speak to you right now, simply move to the next. Take what meets you in this season, and if needed, revisit others later as your situation shifts or changes.

The next thing I want to share is a simple idea called "habit stacking." Before you begin each day's devotional, taking a few moments for deep, intentional breathing can help release tension in your body and settle your mind and nervous system. When you've been through extreme stress or trauma, healing often requires intentionality. This small pause can help you engage more fully with the messages God has for you in these pages.

For this, box breathing is an easy, helpful method:

1. Inhale deeply through your nose for the count of four.
2. Hold your breath for the count of four.
3. Exhale through your mouth for the count of four.
4. Hold again for the count of four.

Visualize making a box, with each side equal in length, as you breathe. Inhale. Hold. Exhale. Hold. You can slightly adjust the count as needed, as long as each side stays the same. I personally like to imagine a relaxing place while breathing—a calm beach, a quiet mountain top, anywhere that brings peace.

Deep breathing is a simple way to help reset our nervous system, especially during stressful seasons. It can help our minds move from reaction to reflection and allow our bodies to release the tension they've been carrying, creating space to be present and fully engaged.

Finally, I want to invite you to find a quiet place to engage with what you find here. Allow God access to your heart and mind. I know how hard it can be at times to carve out this intentional space, but if you can, allow yourself this time, seeking His peace and guidance as you read. Distractions will always be there, but you deserve this time to seek the clarity God has waiting for you.

FOUR TYPES OF MARRIAGES

Now, before we begin, I want to share something I pray will help you as you seek clarity in your marriage or relationship. One of the most common struggles women share with me is how confusing it is to know the true state of their marriage. I remember wrestling with similar questions: "Were our issues common to every marriage, or was I dealing with something more—something beyond routine challenges?" Many women carry this same unspoken confusion, unsure if what they're experiencing is normal or something more.

So, I hope this simple four-tiered framework, inspired in part by several models I encountered while working through my own marital struggles, helps you find clarity.[1,2,3]

If you're just noticing something is not quite right in your marriage, or maybe something feels horribly wrong, it can feel a little like Saul walking on the road to Damascus—like your scales are starting to fall off.

Many women go through a stage where they begin to search and research for answers. Sometimes it can become an all-consuming fire to figure out how to get out of the pain that is happening inside a marriage. So, I want to ease a bit of that here in the beginning of our time together.

We'll start by making some distinctions between the different types of marriages that exist. Every marriage faces challenges. These can range from communication breakdowns, financial stress, busy schedules all the way to deeper patterns of neglect and harm. Not all struggles are the same, and as such, not all warrant the same response.

While no two marriages are alike, because no two people are exactly alike, there are many commonalities between patterns found in marriage. For the sake of clarity, I've grouped marriages into four broad categories, based on the level of safety, connection, and coordination between partners: The "Uncoordinated" marriage, the "Unfulfilled" marriage, the "Undiagnosed and Untreated" marriage, and the "Unsafe and Unsustainable" marriage.

I've done this not because every marriage fits neatly into one of these four categories, but because many women are walking through very confusing dynamics. So anywhere we can simplify the chaos, it helps in making informed decisions.

Below you'll find the four categories in more detail, so you can begin to sense where your marriage might fall on the spectrum.

Category 1: The Uncoordinated Marriage:

"We're not always in sync—but we love each other and keep trying."

This is a marriage where the couple clearly loves and respects one another, but isn't coordinated in certain areas—maybe it's your communication style, or one of you is a planner and the other one is more spontaneous, so you're a bit uncoordinated in your efforts.

You may struggle to stay in sync in everyday life—things like communication, parenting (when both are willing to compromise in healthy ways), finances, household responsibilities, or even cultural differences (when navigated with respect). You may also face normal stressors such as health challenges, busy schedules, or job and moving transitions, but you work through them with mutual respect and effort.

Maybe you feel the need to track every penny and are a great saver, while your spouse is more loose in his financial planning, but isn't reckless or neglectful of it; you just have different styles. While a couple in this marriage may argue or have disagreements from time to time, they know how to do so respectfully and how to repair wisely.

This is a marriage that does not have patterns of unfaithfulness, addictions, destructive and hurtful criticism, deep emotional neglect, or hurtful words or behaviors.

I would say some of the best marriages fall into this category. Much of what a couple in this category struggles with or might find challenging can be compromised on and the marriage remain healthy.

This type of marriage responds well to couples counseling or coaching, date nights, increasing communication skills, marriage retreats, pastoral care, and marriage self-help materials (marriage books, podcasts, courses). This is the marriage that most self-help books on the market today are targeting.

In this type of marriage, a helper, counselor, or coach will focus on looking at both spouses and helping each spouse work on the things that are causing challenges in the marriage.

Category 2: The Unfulfilled Marriage:

"We're rowing the same boat—just not always in the same direction."

In an unfulfilled marriage, a husband and wife are on the same team and clearly love and respect one another, yet they've begun to drift apart. You may wish your husband was more engaged in the things you enjoy. Perhaps after children came along you sensed there was a drift in your emotional connection or felt the romance begin to fade. Maybe you and your husband struggle to stay on the same page with parenting or time with in-laws, yet still respect one another's perspectives.

Maybe he's your polar opposite; you love to go out and socialize and travel and he loves to eat the same meal day in and day out and is a homebody. Or maybe your husband doesn't show interest in the things you do or accomplish, but he is respectful of them. This can even dip into him not understanding what makes you "tick."

A marriage that lacks common ground in interests can leave you feeling unfulfilled or disconnected. However, in this category, it's important to note what isn't present. He never demeans you, belittles you, deeply neglects you, or is unfaithful to you. But, still, you don't hold the same interests, and that can certainly feel unfulfilling.

But there is hope if this is your marriage. There are things that can be done to bring you toward each other because there aren't current or recurrent patterns of harm (i.e. pornography use, adultery, controlling behaviors, gaslighting, deep neglect, or abuse—spiritual, financial, sexual, emotional, or physical).

This type of marriage responds well to all the same things as an uncoordinated marriage, such as couples counseling or coaching, date nights, increasing communication skills, marriage retreats, pastoral care, and marriage self-help materials (marriage books, podcasts, courses), but each spouse may also benefit from some individual counseling or coaching as well.

This type of marriage can slip into the last type if it's not tended to on an individual and a couple's level. Marriage expert John Gottman noted in his book: *The Seven Principles for Making Marriage Work*: "In really good marriages, people are constantly making bids for each other's attention, affection, humor, or support. And those bids are responded to positively."

But when our bids go unnoticed or unattended to for too long, it has the potential to lead to a more deeply unfulfilling marriage, and this can begin to elicit criticism or even bitterness from one or both partners, and that, if left unattended, can slide into the last category. Without intentional time spent together enjoying one another's world, sharing rituals or traditions, and really investing in the lives of each other, a marriage can drift and feel distant or even become deeply neglectful or harmful.

In this type of marriage, a helper, counselor, or coach will focus on looking at both spouses and helping each spouse work on the things that are causing the challenges in the marriage. A couple in this type of marriage may also benefit from individual counseling or help to ensure they are staying healthy and the marriage doesn't slide into the last category.

Category 3: The Undiagnosed or Untreated Marriage:

"Our boat is drifting in a thick fog, one of us sees the storm, but the other doesn't even see the clouds."

This category can be an incredibly difficult place to be. It can feel like walking through a thick fog, but no matter how hard you try, you can't seem to get to the bottom of what's causing the disconnect between you and your husband. There's no overt cruelty, yet the ache in your soul persists—something vital is missing in your marriage, and you're tired of feeling confused by whatever "it" is.

You may feel like you're married to a good man—he doesn't lie, cheat, steal, or engage in seemingly overt abusive behaviors. He's faithful and tries to be a good father—but an emotional connection feels impossible.

You may even feel like you have to coach him on how to meet your most basic emotional needs. Maybe there's no real romance—even a kiss is uncommon—or conversely, sex is the *only* connection you share. Perhaps he lacks the slightest understanding of how to engage with your feelings, shows little emotional affect or empathy, *or* experiences extreme mood shifts that make it feel like everything revolves around him.

No matter how clearly you express your needs or share your hurt, even through tears, he just doesn't "get it." He seems clueless. He might struggle with executive functioning, take things very literally, or be overly blunt in his communication. These traits can lead to frequent misunderstandings and make it difficult for him to relate to others at work and/or at home, leaving you constantly holding the pieces together.

Whatever "it" is has left you feeling emotionally drained and frustrated, while he seems perfectly content with things as they are.

Deep down, you've known something isn't right for far too long. It can feel like you're slowly dying inside without an emotionally attuned partner.

Many women begin to feel hopeless in marriages when a spouse has undiagnosed mental health challenges, neurodivergence, or unresolved trauma. It could be a personality or mood disorder (such as Borderline Personality Disorder, depression, or bipolar disorder), PTSD, C-PTSD, or a form of neurodivergence (such as autism, ADHD, or AuDHD). While this is not an exhaustive list, these conditions and disorders can be challenging even when diagnosed, and potentially even more so when they remain undiagnosed.

Sometimes neither you nor your partner recognizes the underlying issue. Other times, you may begin to suspect something and notice patterns, but he doesn't see it—or doesn't *want* to see it—leaving you feeling isolated, misunderstood, and unsure how to move forward.

In this category, there may or may not be overt or intentional harm, however, the impact can be just as damaging as the last category if the underlying issues aren't identified and addressed. You could experience stress levels similar to those of women in marriages with ongoing, destructive abuse.

The key factor in whether this type of marriage shifts toward becoming an "Unsafe or Unsustainable Marriage" or is able to be repaired is whether or not your husband is willing to admit he has a problem and seek help.

While he may not yet know how to handle the effects of his disorder, mental health condition, or trauma, he must at least be willing and open to understanding what's causing his struggles. Many women in this category, however, know how shut down their husbands become at the slightest hint of counseling or any discussion of a potential "diagnosis," often because it has led to arguments in the past. If this describes your husband, he is likely struggling with more than a neurological or mental health issue—pride, fear, or shame may also be at play, all of which *can* block growth and prevent your marriage from healing.

Marriages in this category benefit first from seeking support for the underlying issue. If your husband is willing, seeking a professional evaluation and diagnosis is a crucial first step. Individual counseling is highly recommended for you as well, as you're likely feeling unseen, unheard, or overwhelmed.

If your husband shows a genuine willingness to seek help for his own harmful patterns first—and stays committed to his own counseling *until there are real, observable changes*—then couples counseling could be considered as a next step. If he doesn't, you will need to truly assess the impact of his problems on your life and your own mental well-being and respond accordingly.

Do note that this category could easily overlap with the next one, depending on the nature and extent of your husband's behaviors related to his underlying condition. These categories are meant only to offer clarity — not to box your marriage into a specific label — but to help you better understand where your challenges may fall and what potential steps toward healing might look like. Try not to get stuck on the categories themselves; instead, focus on the *impact* his behaviors are having on you and your children and on his willingness to take accountability.

Category 4: The Unsafe and Unsustainable Marriage:

"Our boat is sinking, and one of us is fighting to save it, while the other keeps drilling holes in it."

This is a marriage where there's a consistent pattern of harm, and you're not OK. You may not feel emotionally, mentally, or even physically safe. Often, women who find themselves in this category will describe their marriage as destroying them. They may feel as though they are losing their sense of who they truly are.

This category is where we see things like abuse, narcissism, adultery, destructive addictions, or violence occurring within a marriage.

Now, mind you, I have not labeled this marriage unsalvageable or irredeemable. I fully believe in the Word of God, and it tells us that no one is beyond God's reach or repair. So, there have been and can be *some* marriages in this category that experience true restoration. But that depends on two things: the abusive, addicted, or unfaithful spouse's genuine willingness and *proven* ability to change, and your desire to continue with the marriage after experiencing deep hurt and betrayal, which is solely up to you. This is why I said *some*.

The hard, honest truth is that if a man has had a long-standing pattern of abusing or harming his wife or children, and has never shown any inclination to *want* to change, oftentimes that is exactly what happens—he doesn't change.

And in my experience, there are definitely some situations where the wisest and safest choice is to leave immediately. While every situation is unique, a few clear examples include when a spouse has sexually molested a child, consumed child pornography, or been physically violent.

But again, I want to be clear—there are many other forms of abuse that can be equally as destructive. Infidelity, addictions, and emotional, spiritual, sexual, and financial abuse can be just as devastating. And if these patterns are ongoing and unrepentant, separation—whether temporary or permanent—or divorce may be necessary to protect your safety and sanity, and your children.

An unsafe or unsustainable marriage requires a different kind of response than the first two. If a marriage falls into this category, it is *not* recommended that the couple start with couples therapy or couples coaching, non-trauma informed pastoral counseling, or marriage retreats. These things can actually be quite damaging for the spouse who is already being harmed.

In these marriages, the abuse has to be identified and dealt with first and foremost before anything further can take place. This is no longer a "we" issue; it is an abuse issue. And until that is addressed and stopped, no communication tools, date nights, or tips and tricks will ever work.

Lastly, it's important to note that what helps one marriage could increase danger in another, especially when violence, stalking, untreated mental illness, substances, access to weapons, past threats, or coercive control are present. Because I don't know your specific situation, it is always a good idea to filter any advice through the wisdom of a trusted trauma- and abuse-informed professional or community.

Abuse, betrayal, separation, and divorce are deeply nuanced topics. We each bring our own experiences, culture, and faith perspectives into how we see them. I remember how hard it was to sift through advice during my own marriage struggles. I prayed earnestly for God's wisdom, and I encourage you to do the same.

Trust that He will guide you, but also trust the wisdom and discernment He has already given you, especially when it comes to protecting your safety, your sanity, and your children. Listening for God's guidance doesn't always mean waiting for every sign to be perfectly clear. Confusion and chaos are signals, too, and call us to take a step of faith toward health, healing, and safety.

Only you can truly discern the state of your marriage and whether it's safe or wise to remain. My heart in writing this book is to help you name what's true, recognize patterns of harm, and hold fast to the hope God offers—whether you stay or leave.

My prayer for you, long before you ever opened these pages, is that you will find peace here amid your storm. And that something you read will help you take another step toward healing and emotional wholeness—for both you and your children.

Restoring Safety and Clarity

The Cocoon Phase

Think of this season as your cocoon—a sacred, protective space where you can rest under God's covering while He begins restoring your heart and mind. Here, you'll begin to gain clarity about your relationship and restore your sense of safety and sanity. Consider these your first steps on your journey.

In this stage, the butterfly is still a caterpillar with one focus—staying alive. You, too, will need to focus on safety—emotionally, physically, and spiritually. Allow yourself to build a strong foundation through nourishment, self-care, and rest. Just as the caterpillar eats to prepare for its cocoon, you're preparing yourself for the work of transformation, too.

A caterpillar instinctively retreats into its cocoon when it's time for change. You may also feel the need to pull back—not from everything, but from certain people, places, or activities that are draining. Some people may not be equipped to walk with you on this part of your journey. Begin seeking those who can safely support you as you heal and grow.

By now, you've likely begun to sense that the weight you've been carrying is far heavier than you realized. This is a good time to slow down and take on less. This is not weakness, it's wisdom. Protecting your heart and conserving your energy makes room for God to do the deep work of healing.

In this section, you'll learn about God's heart for you, your marriage, and your children. Then you'll begin naming what's true so you can see your situation more clearly.

Day 1
God is Not the Author of Confusion

"God is not the author of confusion but of peace."
1 Corinthians 14:33, NKJV

——*Pause. Take a few deep breaths. Now rest—and abide in Him.*——

If you're reading this, you're likely seeking peace and clarity in your life—specifically in your marriage or in a difficult relationship. This season, and maybe many seasons before this, have likely felt murky, chaotic, and confusing.

I understand. I've been where you are. And I know how painful it can feel. You love God, but at times, you may wonder where He is in the midst of so much pain and heartache. I sure have.

Continuing to learn more about the heart of God has brought me great peace, even in the middle of great suffering. Not the God as described by fallen men and women, maybe not even the God we hear about in our churches each week, but God as *He* describes Himself to be.

A God of love, a God of justice, a God of mercy, a God of righteous anger and sorrow on behalf of those who suffer, and a God of beautiful order and peace.

First Corinthians 14:33 (NKJV) tells us that "God is not the author of confusion but of peace." But here's the funny thing about peace and where *I* have often gotten it wrong: Peace is not the absence of chaos; it's the presence of clarity in the middle of it.

It's finding our calm no matter how fast our world is spinning. It's like Peter locking eyes with the Savior on a stormy sea, about to sink, yet he centers himself on Jesus, seeks His help, and suddenly finds himself walking on the stormy waves and into his Redeemer's arms.

Only a God who can command that the waves be still, a God of order and not of chaos, can bring about this kind of peace in the midst of confusion. And, sweet friend, this is what He wants to do for you, too.

God is not the author of the hurt and pain in your marriage. He would never intentionally harm you. He is not behind the betrayal, the anger, the deception, or the cycles of confusion. Because those things aren't a part of His nature.

I invite you to separate your pain and doubt from God's desires for your life. I invite you to allow yourself to believe that God *does* want good things for you.

God's heart is for all of His daughters to experience emotional, physical, and spiritual safety inside their marriages.

Our marriages are meant to reflect God's abundance of joy and goodness, not an abundance of instability, pain, and uncertainty. I want to encourage you, as you're able, to start trusting God for His abundance and joy in the here and now.

These things are not just for when we reach heaven one day. You can experience peace even during this season of confusion in your marriage. Calm can exist in your heart even if you don't know what your next steps will be.

This is just the beginning, the start of a new chapter. One where you get to choose calm and peace no matter how high the waves are. As we walk this journey together, I pray God brings you one step closer each day to the clarity only He can give.

You don't have to figure out every detail today. Just breathe. And take the *one* next step He places in front of you. As you do, He promises to be right beside you.

Prayer:

Dear God, I lay the chaos and confusion of my marriage at Your feet. I will choose to reach for Your hand each and every time I feel like I am sinking beneath the waves. I choose to believe You are not the author of the pain I'm experiencing, and that You want good things for me and my children. Help me to have clarity about my marriage. Thank you, God, for Your promises and for who You are and how You are going to help me. Amen.

Reflection:

If you could release one doubt, one fear, or one lie about God's heart for you, what would it be? And what truth about His character could you hold onto instead?

Day 2
God's Heart is for the Oppressed

*"The righteous cry out, and the Lord hears,
and delivers them out of all their troubles."*
Psalm 34:17, NKJV

——*Pause. Take a few deep breaths. Now rest—and abide in Him.*——

Scripture is filled with verses referencing God's heart and concern for the poor, the needy, and the oppressed.

Throughout the Psalms, the books of the prophets, as well as many other places, we see a picture of a God who deeply cares for those who have been wronged. It's clear God's heart is drawn to the vulnerable.

His heart aches when our hearts ache. He is deeply moved when His children experience injustice or abuse, and His righteous anger burns against the cruelty that causes His daughters to despair. God is not indifferent to the heartache and harm you've endured.

Perhaps in your experience, though, it hasn't felt this way. Maybe the Bible has been used to keep you silent, compliant, or trapped in harm's way. Sweet friend, if that's the case, please hear me when I say, that is not from the heart of God. His Word is not meant to bind you to abuse but rather to set you free to live in His love.

Psalm 9:9 (KJV) promises: "The Lord will be a refuge for the oppressed." In Deuteronomy 10:18, we're told He will be a defender of the fatherless and the widows. In Proverbs 11:1, it tells us God hates deceit, and in Isaiah 1:17 (NKJV), He commands all people to "learn to do good... seek justice, rebuke the oppressor."

In Malachi 2:16, we see God rebuking men who are being unfaithful to their wives.

> "The man who hates and divorces his wife," says the Lord, the God of Israel, "does violence to the one he should protect," says the Lord Almighty. So be on your guard, and do not be unfaithful.

While some versions of the Bible read "God hates divorce," a more accurate translation is "For the man who *hates* and divorces his wife." This is how it's written in the ancient Greek version, the language spoken in Jesus's time.

In context, God is not simply saying He hates divorce—though it certainly grieves His heart. He is saying He hates the violence, betrayal, and treachery that leads to it.

Marriage is never more important to God than the two people inside of it. Nor is it more important than your children, who will either witness a marriage that reflects Christ or one that reflects the lies of the enemy.

God's standard for marriage is clear:

> Husbands, love your wives, just as Christ also loved the church and gave Himself for her. So, husbands ought to love their own wives as their own bodies; he who loves his wife loves himself. For no one ever hated his own flesh, but nourishes and cherishes it, just as the Lord does the church. For we are members of His body, of His flesh and of His bones (Ephesians 5:25, 28-29, NKJV).

God's heart is always for the oppressed. Yes, He longs for your husband to repent because He wants to see him in heaven one day—but this doesn't mean He overlooks his repeated sins.

His Word promises us He will avenge the oppressed and judge the wicked. And for those who have been crushed, He offers comfort and His nearness: "The Lord is close to the brokenhearted and saves those who are crushed in spirit" (Psalm 34:18, NIV).

Dear sister, if you have been told God values your marriage above your safety or sanity, please know this: God values you. He is your Refuge, your Defender, and your Healer. He would never desire to keep you bound to harm or abuse but longs to lead you into freedom and wholeness.

Prayer:

Dear Father, thank You for being a God who sees my pain. Please help me to know Your heart for me and my children. Teach me what it means for You to be my Defender. Help me identify any lies I may have believed about Your character and replace them with truth. Protect my heart and mind as I take the steps toward clarity and healing. And surround me with Your presence, Your people, and Your peace. Amen.

Reflection:

Do you believe God values your (and your children's) safety and emotional well-being as much as He values your marriage? Have you believed that enduring harm is somehow holy or that suffering is simply a part of your calling as a wife? Is God inviting you to see holiness not as enduring pain but as the pursuit of wholeness in Him?

Day 3
The Shepherd Who Protects

*"I am the good shepherd. The good shepherd
gives His life for the sheep."*
John 10:11, NKJV

——*Pause. Take a few deep breaths. Now rest—and abide in Him.*——

Jesus is a Protective Shepherd. He leaves the ninety-nine to go after the one who is lost. That's the Savior we serve. He would go to ends of the Earth to protect your heart, even leaving behind everyone else to make sure you're not alone, abused, frightened, neglected, or devastated.

He cares as much for the safety of our souls as a shepherd would over the safety of his flock. He longs to guide us back onto the path toward safe, green pastures where He can better oversee our steps. But that same Shepherd, who is gentle toward His sheep, becomes fierce toward the predators that threaten them.

That's the Savior we see in Scripture. Jesus was tender to the brokenhearted as He walked the dusty roads of this world. He healed the wounded and drew near to the oppressed. But that same Jesus overturned tables when He saw God's children being exploited. He called wrong, wrong. He called deceitful men "a brood of vipers" and "whitewashed tombs" (Matthew 12:34, Matthew 23:27, NKJV).

He deeply cares about you and your little ones and would never want you to suffer at the hands of someone else's sin. He didn't condone that kind of suffering during His ministry in the flesh — and He doesn't now.

This matters because too often, as wives, we've been taught it is an honor to suffer quietly — that submission to pain is somehow sacred. We're told that if we endure long enough, we might "win" our husbands to the Lord.

But Scripture never commands us to enable sin or endure harm — and condoning sin doesn't win anyone to God. Yes, 1 Peter 3 encourages a gentle spirit toward an unbelieving spouse, but it never asks wives to surrender their safety or dignity. That's not the nature of a loving, protective Shepherd. He does not sacrifice one soul to cover another's wrongdoing.

If that were true, Jesus would not have called out injustice and hypocrisy while He walked the Earth — He would have simply endured it. But He didn't. Jesus defended the oppressed and resisted evil up to the moment His Father called Him to endure the ultimate suffering. But His sacrifice was never about enabling sin, but defeating it once and for all. It was redemptive — not soul-destroying.

When God says we *will* suffer but to count it a delight, He is referring to a suffering that brings *glory* to His name. To suffer for the name of Christ *is* an honor for the believer. But to suffer for the enabling of sins isn't.

God created marriage to exalt *His* glory, as a reflection of the marriage between Christ and His bride, the church. We are told our husbands are to love us as He loved the church. Christ would never harm His bride.

God didn't create marriage to make martyrs out of wives while condoning the behavior that harms, neglects, or abuses them. That would not glorify Him, but distort His image. And that's not the nature of a loving God or His Son—our protective Shepherd.

Sweet friend, I pray you can rest in this truth today: Your Shepherd is not calling you to endure harm, but He is inviting you to experience His care and protection.

Prayer:

Dear Father, thank You for pursuing me with Your tenderness and love. Thank You that Your heart is for me to heal and not to be harmed. Teach me to rest in Your care and help me to trust in Your protection. Please defend me against anything that is not of You and that could harm my soul. And show me the difference between suffering that honors Your name and any pain that You never intended for me to bear. Please guard and protect my heart, and my children's hearts, and help me to continue growing in clarity in my marriage. Amen.

Reflection:

Have you confused Christ-like love with enabling sin? Knowing that Jesus deeply cares for your safety and wholeness, does this change your view of His love for you? How might it change your view of your husband's wrong behaviors toward you?

Day 4
Grace Upon Grace

"My grace is sufficient for you, for my power is made perfect in weakness."
2 Corinthians 12:9

——*Pause. Take a few deep breaths. Now rest—and abide in Him.*——

John 1:14 calls Jesus "The Word [that] became flesh and made his dwelling among us." And then it finishes by giving this description of Jesus: "We have seen his glory, the glory of the one and only Son, who came from the Father, *full of grace and truth*" (emphasis added).

Jesus is not just our protector, our friend, and our guide—He is also our example. Did you notice in this verse that it says He is *full* of grace and truth? When we feel we've stumbled or fallen, He is there *full* of grace to urge us forward and to give us hope.

I remember many nights when arguments from earlier in the day would drag into the wee hours of the morning, leaving me exhausted and desperate for sleep. Most of the time I would just give in—wave the white flag so the conflict would stop and I could get some rest.

But one night, my nervous system gave out before I could agree, and I snapped and yelled back. The moment the words left my mouth, I was shocked. And then I just fell apart, as though years of stress had come flooding out, messy sobs and all. I was a sleep-deprived mess! I felt so ashamed—but also strangely relieved. Even there, in my mess, God's grace met me.

Sweet friend, Jesus doesn't fault us if, in a heated moment, we slip and raise our voice. While it may not be our finest moment, it's a normal reaction. This type of reaction, though not ideal, is our body and soul sounding the alarm that something is deeply wrong and crying out for relief.

What is *not* normal is to be continually demeaned, spoken down to, mocked, yelled at, or deeply neglected. Anyone would crack under that kind of relenting storm. It's normal to lose our composure from time to time, because it is *not* normal to consistently endure mistreatment.

Maybe, unlike me, you've never raised your voice, but you've resorted to the silent treatment, or shut down emotionally, or longed for an escape. Jesus knows the stress your heart has been under, and He sees the wrongs that are happening in your marriage. And He is *full* of grace toward you. "My grace is sufficient for you, for my power is made perfect in weakness" (2 Corinthians 12:9).

When you are at your weakest, don't lose heart. Jesus doesn't. In those moments when your nervous system can't take one more wrong, when your heart is aching and your mind can't hold one more ounce of dysfunction, when you react in ways you wished you hadn't, Jesus doesn't lose His patience with you. He draws near. In that very weakness, His power is made perfect, and His grace covers you completely.

We also need to learn how to have grace on ourselves in these hard moments. Reacting to dysfunction or abuse is different than *being* abusive. Have grace on yourself for how far you've come. I can only imagine what you've survived. I'm sure it hasn't been easy, or you likely wouldn't be reading this.

Remember: Your story is not defined by the moments where you stumble but by your continual choice to allow His grace to be sufficient for you.

His grace is strong enough to cover your tears, your missteps, and your exhaustion. It's powerful enough to carry you forward. Sweet friend, you are not alone in this. His grace is sufficient for you—one day at a time.

Prayer:

Dear Heavenly Father, thank You for Your grace and Your love. My heart is weary and raw. Help me to have grace on myself as I navigate the trials in my marriage. Help me to have Your heart and to protect my soul. Help me to love but not allow anyone to continually wear me down. And give me the wisdom to know how to do both. Amen.

Reflection:

In the past week, where have you felt stretched, exhausted, or overwhelmed? How did you respond to yourself in those moments, and how might you give grace to yourself instead?

Day 5
Truth Telling

"The Word became flesh and made his dwelling among us. We have seen his glory, the glory of the one and only Son, who came from the Father, full of grace and truth."

John 1:14

——*Pause. Take a few deep breaths. Now rest—and abide in Him.*——

God calls us to follow His example and to strive to be more like His Son. Jesus was loving, kind, patient, merciful—*and*, John 1:14 also tells us, He was full of truth. In fact, as He walked in this broken world, He never shied away from the hard truths He needed to speak. And He calls us to do the same.

The very first step of healing any emotional wound is to name it. But I know how hard that can be when we ourselves don't even understand what's happening. Often the patterns are hidden, inconsistent, and confusing—and leave us second guessing ourselves. So, owning the truth takes time and wisdom. But I encourage you, over the following days and weeks, to allow the truth to come to the light and not shy away from it.

And one truth we have to face is that not everyone is going to protect our hearts. In fact, some people are even going to harm them.

While this is easier to grapple with when it's a stranger, it can be brutally painful to reconcile when it's our spouse, the very person who vowed to love and honor us.

I had to grieve this in my own story. For years I desperately clung to the belief that my husband would never hurt me. But when the pain and chaos didn't stop, I started to cling to another misbelief: My husband never *meant* to hurt me.

Eventually, though, I had to face a very hard truth: If someone keeps wounding me, regardless of their intentions or even their attempts to change, then stopping simply isn't a priority for them. And admitting that was excruciating.

I wanted so badly to be "enough" for him to *want* to change. But the truth remained—I wasn't. And that truth stung deep down in my soul. Yet even as I sat with that pain, Jesus whispered to my heart, "It's not about you. You have always been enough." He was teaching me that my worth was, and still is, found in Him, not in my husband—or his choices.

It wasn't until I was willing to admit the truth about my marriage and name what was happening that I found true peace and clarity. The Bible tells us that when we know and accept the truth, "the truth will set us free" (John 8:32). It did for me. I hope it will for you, too.

Because the truth is, whether your husband means to cause you pain or not, if he is hurting you, and doing so repeatedly and deeply, it leaves scars. At the end of the day, it's not about intention—it's about the impact it leaves on your soul.

But the good news is that the same Jesus who is filled with truth won't shy away from your story. He will be there to hold your hand as you walk through this hard chapter in your life—and will never let you go.

Prayer:

Dear Heavenly Father, thank You for loving me and wanting me to know the truth. Please hold me as I begin to open my eyes to the patterns that are happening in my marriage. Hold my heart, because I may not want to see what You have to show me. Even still, help me not to shy away. Help me to heal, help my children to heal and help us all to walk in Your truth. Amen.

Reflection:

What have you been avoiding or overlooking in your marriage and why? What are the consequences of honestly acknowledging them and are you ready to take the steps toward healing?

Day 6
Naming the Truth Isn't Unfairly Judging

*"Yes, just as you can identify a tree by its fruit,
so you can identify people by their actions."*
Matthew 7:20, NLT

——Pause. Take a few deep breaths. Now rest—and abide in Him.——

Often in Christian circles people are quick to advise you to avoid "judging" your husband. They may say things like, "Well, we all sin," or "Who are we to judge?" And while this may sound biblical on the surface, it isn't complete.

Jesus says we *are* to acknowledge the fruit we see—or don't see—in the lives of others. Naming the harmful patterns in your marriage is truth telling and is called discernment. Discernment and hypocritical judging are two very different things. We're commanded to be discerning.

That's different from the Pharisaical judgment Jesus was referring to in Matthew 7:1-5. When Jesus said, "Judge not, that ye be not judged. For with what judgment ye judge, ye shall be judged," He isn't saying don't notice evil and don't call it out. He's saying make sure that same evil isn't controlling our own hearts before we do so.

In the verse after this one, He says *before* (note this word) we attempt to take the speck from our brother's eye, we should remove the beam from our own. He doesn't say don't attempt to remove the speck; He simply gives us an action to do first.

He wants to make sure we're not doing exactly what the Pharisees were known for doing: overlooking our own heart condition while trying to control or look down on others. We can see this more clearly in Matthew 7:5, when Jesus plainly starts with these words: "Thou hypocrite." In these verses, He was addressing anyone who lets hypocrisy reign in their heart.

Jesus isn't condemning judgment here, but rather us judging others with an outrageous standard that we ourselves wouldn't want to be judged by.

While we are called to love *all* people unconditionally, we are not called to unconditionally approve of *all* the things they do. We know this because in the very same chapter Jesus goes on to say in great lengths that we "can identify [others] by their fruit. That is, by the way they act." He then says that "a bad tree bears bad fruit" (Matthew 7:15-23, NLT).

Clearly if we're called to identify others by their fruits then we must be using some kind of discernment or "judgment" to do so.

Sweet friend, if your husband is repeating patterns in your marriage that belittle you, harm you, control you, or strip away your freedoms and identity, you are not wrong to name what is happening. Yes, we all make mistakes, but repeated, unrepented harm isn't just a mistake—it's abuse. It is good, and even holy, to call bad fruit by its real name.

God calls us to use discernment in all our relationships, especially with our spouses, because they have the closest access to our hearts. Don't let anyone dissuade you from truthfully naming what's happening in your marriage.

In the days ahead, I'm going to share some things that may feel hard, even scary, to see for what they truly are. They might even stir emotions you would rather not feel: grief, sorrow, anger, fear. But I encourage you, don't shy away. You're not sinful for naming the truth. You're not "judging" your husband with a condemning spirit. You're simply practicing the discernment Christ calls us to have—and calling the fruit you see by its right name.

Sweet friend, you have a part to play—to bravely see the truth and then take the needed steps to deal with the truths He shows you. I promise you, though it may feel hard, doing this is where hope begins. And Jesus has a great hope and future for you.

Prayer:

Dear Heavenly Father, please hold me in this process of seeing and naming the truth in my marriage. I know You understand the weight of betrayal and pain. And I trust that You would never open my eyes to something You didn't intend to walk beside me through and protect my heart from. Help me to trust You in this daily. Amen.

Reflection:

Have you held back from naming what's happening in your marriage out of fear of "judging" your husband? Have you told yourself you have no right to speak up because you make mistakes, too? What might discernment look like in this situation?

Day 7
Naming What's Hard to Name: The Cycles

"The people walking in darkness have seen a great light; on those living in the land of deep darkness a light has dawned."
Isaiah 9:2

———*Pause. Take a few deep breaths. Now rest—and abide in Him.*———

Years ago, before I had the words to describe what was happening in my marriage, it felt like I was living in the dark. I was stumbling around, bumping into the same painful problems, unable to find the light switch to illuminate the issues.

Yet, in the middle of it all, God reminded me that darkness was not His end: "The people walking in darkness have seen a great light; on those living in the land of deep darkness a light has dawned" (Isaiah 9:2). He was faithful and began to answer my prayer—"Lord, please show me what is happening"—in an unexpected way.

Providentially, I attended a training for missionaries to learn how to better serve those who were hurting. I believe God brought me to that training because, though we were missionaries at the time, *I* was the one hurting.

One phrase from the seminar has stayed with me ever since: "We have to name what's happening, in order to claim what's happening, so that we can begin to tame what's happening." Though not always as simply as it sounds, simply put: "Name it. Claim it. Tame it."

In unsafe and unsustainable marriages, often there are repeating cycles, filled with confusion and tension. Tension builds, you feel like you're walking on eggshells, and then something triggers your spouse, and there's either an explosion, an argument, or maybe the silent treatment used as punishment.

This is often followed by a cool-down period, or what's called the honeymoon phase, where apologies, love bombing, or maybe just calm, neutral behavior give you hope that things can change. So, you forgive (again) and try to move forward, often telling yourself that love "keeps no record of wrongs" (1 Corinthians 13:5).

But remember, sweet friend, this isn't about past wrongs—it's about recurring, current patterns of wrongdoing. There is a difference, and it matters.

I lived in this cycle for years—tension building, apologies, attempts at getting help, counseling, prayer. But nothing broke the cycle. Then a counselor helped me name what was happening—it was like the scales fell from my eyes, and I could finally see the patterns clearly. And once I did, I couldn't unsee it. Many women I've worked with go through a similar experience.

If you find yourself in this place, don't be afraid to step out of the darkness and into the light. The light is where Jesus can bring healing.

The Israelites lived for generations under the oppression of the Pharaohs. They were trapped in cycles that seemed impossible to escape, until God sent someone to lead them to freedom. What must have seemed hopeless was not beyond God's power to redeem. God wants to bring you out of the darkness and unending cycles, too.

But even as they were headed toward freedom, they had times where they wanted to go back to the dysfunction they had known, because it had been "home" for so long. Don't be surprised if this happens to you, too. When we live in dysfunction long enough, it can start to feel familiar, like home. But keep pressing forward toward healing and freedom.

Jesus said that when you "know the truth, the truth will set you free" (John 8:32). Yes, the truth can be painful—but it's the first step toward healing. Naming the cycles in your marriage is the first step to taming them. And God wants to guide you through this process with His strength.

As Isaiah chapter 9 reminds us, once the light dawns, God brings freedom and joy, and burdens fall away. Step by step, in His strength, the cycles can lose their power as His light replaces the darkness. God wants this for you, too.

We can't control whether our marriage changes or force our spouse to change. All we can control is ourselves—and we can choose truth. We can take the brave step to name what's happening, take ownership of our boundaries, and begin walking toward freedom.

Prayer:

Dear Heavenly Father, help me not to fear what You reveal. Please open the door so the light can come in, and when it does, help me not to shy away. Amen.

Reflection/Action Step:

Write down any cycles or repeating patterns you notice in your marriage. Over the coming days and weeks, continue logging them in your journal and keep it in a private place. This can help you see how long the patterns have been occurring and prevent minimizing or forgetting their impact. Simply notice, record, and allow God to bring clarity and light.

Day 8
Naming What's Hard to Name: Emotional Abuse

"So do not fear, for I am with you, do not be dismayed, for I am your God. I will strengthen you and help you: I will uphold you with my righteous right hand."
Isaiah 41:10, NKJV

———*Pause. Take a few deep breaths. Now rest—and abide in Him.*———

After years of sitting with women as they recount their stories, I'm convinced—emotional abuse is one of the more insidious and quietly destructive forms of abuse. It doesn't just wound, it destroys the soul.

I can't count the number of women I've heard say, "I think I'm going crazy." Not because the abuse is obvious—but because it isn't. They tell me, "My husband is a good man, He doesn't hit me or yell, but I feel like I'm dying inside." Slowly, as they share, the picture starts to clear. He's emotionally detached, controlling, or cold, or she feels unseen, small, and neglected.

The most common phrase I hear is "I know he doesn't mean to hurt me." And my reply is always the same: Emotional abuse isn't about intention—it's about impact. It's like taking two trees: one slowly dies from neglect while the other is consumed in a forest fire. Different causes, but same results.

For Christian women especially, the fear of naming what's happening can feel paralyzing, especially if they've been taught the only "real" forms of abuse or injury are a black eye or an affair. Emotional abuse is deeply insidious because it feels so subjective. It's difficult to name and even harder to prove. It feels like it's just your word against his, especially if he insists *you* are the problem.

There's no tangible evidence like with other forms of harm—no other woman, no visible marks, only your emotional reactions. This kind of abuse quietly destroys you from the inside out—where no one else can see.

Every couple has differences of opinion and all partners make mistakes. We're human. But, abuse is different. It's not having an off day or one heated argument; it's a pattern of ongoing control, dismissal, and a power imbalance that creates an environment that lacks peace and mutual respect.

It might look like your partner telling you that you're crazy when you catch him in a lie—gaslighting you until you doubt your own reality.

It might look like your partner hurting you, then becoming angry when you express your pain, turning the story around so you become the offender and he becomes the victim. This is a pattern referred to as DARVO (Deny, Attack, Reverse Offender and Victim).

It might look like cycles of agitation, frustration, outbursts, punishing you with the silent treatment, emotional neglect, or long "sermons" where he corners you in an effort to force his views on you.

It could even look like your husband withholding emotional or sexual intimacy as a way of punishing you when he doesn't get his way.

He may seem like Mr. Wonderful at church, yet behind closed doors he becomes a totally different person. Like Dr. Jekyll and Mister Hyde, he leaves you walking on eggshells in your own home.

At its core, emotional abuse confuses, entangles, and erodes your sense of reality. It leaves you feeling small, exhausted, overlooked, unheard, and unloved. Like you've stumbled into a dark hole and can't find your way out.

You're not crazy, too sensitive, or imagining things. If these patterns are present and don't stop especially after you've expressed how much they hurt you, this is not love, even if apologies, or moments of fun and kindness are mixed in. This is abuse—and abuse destroys intimacy. When you've been repeatedly lied to, gaslit, spoken down to, and smothered with control, eventually you no longer trust—not your partner who is hurting you, not yourself, and sometimes not even God.

It's like a slow-moving cancer, quietly spreading throughout every part of your life. Often it has already done a great deal of damage before you're able to identify it. The pain lives in your body, the stress hijacks your nervous system, and the confusion leaves your mind reeling.

God doesn't want you to live in darkness. That's why naming what is happening in your marriage is so important. When you step into the light, it brings clarity. And once you begin naming the truth, it's important to understand one of the biggest lies that can keep women stuck.

Many abusive men say, "I don't mean to hurt you," or "I lash out because I'm hurting." This may sound sincere, even tragic—but it is a deflection of responsibility.

While an abusive person may genuinely feel hurt and pain, that doesn't give them the right to lash out at others because of their pain. And all too often, I've seen abusive people use their pain to justify their harmful actions, instead of seeking help and healing.

Yes, your partner may have had a terrible childhood or be experiencing stress at work, but his brokenness does *not* give him the right to break you.

Jesus never excused sin based on emotional wounds. He showed compassion, yes—but always called for repentance, not rationalization. The truth is, many of us have complicated pasts, but we don't all use them to harm others. Your partner can do better, if he chooses to.

Jesus healed many—but He always left people with a choice: "Do you want to be well?" (John 5:6)

If your spouse does not want to be well—if he chooses control, blame, and manipulation—then your love cannot reach him. That is not your fault. Healing is a choice. Abuse is a choice.

God is love so He would never condone abuse—ever. Allow Him to give you *His* strength as you walk this journey. I know how scary it can feel to start admitting these things—I truly do. Ask God to hold your heart as you begin to acknowledge the truth. And then, with His help, start taking the steps toward healing, safety, and truth.

"So do not fear, for I am with you, do not be dismayed, for I am your God. I will strengthen you and help you: I will uphold you with my righteous right hand" (Isaiah 41:10, NKJV).

Prayer:

Dear Heavenly Father, my heart is heavy from the pain and hurt I've experienced in my marriage. Please hold me close and help me to clearly see all I'm experiencing. Bring it into Your light and give me the wisdom and courage to discern my next steps. Amen.

Reflection:

Emotional abuse can show up in many ways, and sometimes it can be hard to identify it on your own. To help, I have an Emotional Abuse Questionnaire, which you can use as a tool to notice recurring patterns, reflect on your experiences, and begin to name what's happening in your marriage. It can be found here: www.darahashlie.com/resources.

Day 9
Naming What's Hard to Name: Verbal Abuse

"Death and life are in the power of the tongue."
Proverbs 18:21, NKJV

—— *Pause. Take a few deep breaths. Now rest—and abide in Him.* ——

Words are meant to build us up, comfort our souls, and breathe new life into our being. God spoke—and there was *life*. This was His design from the very beginning.

But all too often, words are used to harm, destroy, and demean. And when this happens, it chips away at the very fabric of our souls—little by little. It leaves dark, hidden stains on our hearts as we internalize the hurtful words and begin to believe them. Over time, they destroy our self-worth and leave us flinching, waiting for the next barrage.

It might look like someone continually criticizing you or taking your most intimate insecurities and weaponizing them against you.

It might sound like yelling, swearing, or making back-handed comments to hurt you.

At their worst, words are used to threaten you or bring death and hopelessness to your soul.

If someone calls you a horrible name and then blames you—"I don't know why you're acting that way; it was just a joke"—they're lacking emotional maturity and do not have your best interest at heart.

And if this is your husband, first, I want to say how sorry I am. No one should ever speak to you in these ways. Especially not a man, who stands in the role God designed to edify and build you up—as Christ does for the church (Ephesians 5:25).

The Bible has quite a bit to say about this.

Proverbs 18:21 (NKJV) says: "Death and life are in the power of the tongue." If words continually bring death instead of life—that's destructive.

Proverbs 12:18 (ESV) says: "There is one whose rash words are like sword thrusts, but the tongue of the wise brings healing." Someone who truly loves you will use their words to heal you, not harm you.

Ephesians 1:29 (NLT) says, "Don't use foul or abusive language. Let everything you say be good and helpful, so that your words will be an encouragement to those who hear them." And again, God addresses this: "But now you yourselves are to put off all these: anger, wrath, malice, blasphemy, filthy language out of your mouth" (Colossians 3:8, NKJV).

When a husband refuses to "put off" these behaviors and chooses instead to speak in hateful ways, God says: "Everyone who is angry with his brother will be liable to judgment" (Matthew 5:22, NKJV).

Your heart matters to God. Your husband's heart matters to God.

God doesn't want your husband separating himself from Him by continually using his words to wound you. And He doesn't want you losing your God-given identity by believing the lies being spoken over you.

You're not "too sensitive" or "overreacting" for being hurt by cruel words. And you're not at fault for the rudeness or meanness he chooses to unleash. A husband who cannot bridle his tongue is not walking in Christ-like servanthood.

If you find yourself enduring cycles of this, followed by apologies or brief seasons of kind words, name it for what it is—abuse. Because true love "does not behave rudely, does not seek its own, is not provoked, thinks no evil" (1 Corinthians 13:5, NKJV).

Healing begins the moment you start to believe God's words are stronger than what's been said about you. And God has never uttered one word meant to make you feel unworthy.

Lean into God's heart today. Set a boundary around your soul. It's good—and holy—to protect yourself and not allow anyone, especially your husband, to speak to you in ways that destroy.

Prayer:

Heavenly Father, my heart hurts over the words that have been said about me. Heal my soul and help me to uproot any misbeliefs that have taken root. Give me the courage to start setting safe boundaries and surround me with Your presence and peace.

Reflection:

What boundaries can you set to protect your heart from the things being said to you? Write down Scripture verses that counteract any lies you've believed.

Note: If your spouse is prone to violence, some boundaries may unintentionally escalate violence. So, it is best to seek guidance from a trusted professional as you explore what boundaries might look like in your relationship.

Day 10
Naming What's Hard to Name: Physical Abuse

"The Lord tests the righteous, but the wicked and the one who loves violence His soul hates."

Psalm 11:5, NKJV

———*Pause. Take a few deep breaths. Now rest—and abide in Him.*———

There is nothing good that comes from being physically violent or intimidating toward another person. Proverbs 11:29 says: "He who troubles his own house will inherit the wind." Dear sister, if this is what you're experiencing, it is time to leave.

Physical abuse is not limited to bruises and broken bones. It is also being physically threatened. Many abusers know exactly how far to go to scare and intimidate without ever leaving a mark—that does not mean it isn't physical abuse.

If your spouse repeatedly restrains you, blocks your exit, throws things, punches holes in walls, or harms your pets, he is trying to scare and control you, even if he does not hit you directly. And often, when these behaviors occur, the violence escalates over time.

If this is your husband, know this: He does not have the spirit of Christ living in Him. Jesus would never frighten you. God has very strong feelings about violence and anyone who commits it. Scripture says He *hates* the one who perpetrates violence (Psalm 11:5).

The Bible tells us God is the same yesterday, today, and always. He is the God of both the Old and the New Testaments. And in the Old Testament, God gives laws to protect the vulnerable from violence and harm (see Exodus 21 and Deuteronomy 22).

In the New Testament, we see Jesus protecting the woman caught in adultery from being stoned and exposing the hypocrisy of her accusers. And just listen to how He explains His mission in Luke 4:18:

> The spirit of the Lord is on me, because He has anointed me to proclaim good news to the poor. He has sent me to proclaim freedom for the prisoners and recovery of sight for the blind, to set the oppressed free.

Jesus stands near you now—calling out your husband's sin, shielding you from harm, and calling you to freedom. Don't be afraid to take His hand and move toward safety—your life, your peace, and your children's well-being depend on it. God did not create you to live in fear, but in His perfect love.

Prayer:

Thank You for seeing me and my children. And thank You for showing me just how important our safety is. Help me not to minimize what has been happening in my home. Please give me the courage to take steps to get to safety. I long for freedom from the fear and chaos in my home—surround us with Your peace as only You can. Amen.

Reflection:

Are there boundaries you need to put into place immediately to protect yourself and your children? Who are the safe people you can reach out to for help? What next step can you take to make sure you are safe?

* I have provided a link to a Safety Plan in the back of this devotional. I encourage you to fill it out and keep it somewhere only you can access and give a copy to a safe and trusted person. Consider it not just a plan, but an act of honoring the worth that God has placed on your life and a way to protect the precious gift He has entrusted to you.

Day 11
Naming What's Hard to Name: Sexual Abuse

"Whoever commits adultery with a woman lacks understanding; he who does so destroys his own soul. Wounds and dishonor he will get, and his reproach will not be wiped away."
Proverbs 6:32-33, NKJV

———*Pause. Take a few deep breaths. Now rest—and abide in Him.*———

If your husband is unfaithful, whether in his heart, through hidden sexual sin, or in his actions toward you, it will rightfully cause pain and breed mistrust.

Proverbs 25:19 (KJV) says it this way: "Confidence in an unfaithful man in a time of trouble is like a broken tooth and a foot out of joint."

That's a striking image. A broken tooth can cause pain that shifts from dull to sharp, flaring up every time you try to use it. And a foot out of joint leaves you unable to walk without agony. Both are injuries that make the simplest movement unbearable. These are things that demand our attention.

In the same way, when someone we love betrays our trust through lies, infidelity, sexual sins, or viewing pornography, it creates a wound that cannot simply be brushed aside. God understands this kind of pain. He is showing us it's natural and right to feel deep pain and uncertainty when our trust is betrayed.

You can't lean on someone whose actions have made them untrustworthy—it's like trying to stand on a dislocated foot. They are no longer a firm foundation.

Proverbs 6:32-33 (NKJV) says a man who commits adultery "lacks understanding… and destroys his own soul… and his reproach won't be wiped away."

Sexual abuse in marriage takes many forms. It may look like being pressured, coerced, guilted, or forced into sexual acts you don't want to participate in. It may involve withholding sex and affection as a form of punishment. It may involve being body shamed, manipulated into sex, or treated as an object to meet your husband's sexual desires. It can also show up in secret spaces—soliciting escorts, viewing pornography, or committing adultery.

Any time sex is used as a means of control or manipulation and disregards your will, it is abuse. God does not minimize sexual sin or the harm it causes. Trauma specialists confirm what Scripture alludes to—betrayal trauma is one of the deepest forms of traumas. It can shatter our sense of safety, violate the sacred bond of trust, and leave deep emotional scars that can affect our ability to trust others and even ourselves in the future.

Dear one, if this is your story, I hope you can hear this: What is happening to you is not your fault. God never asks a wife to submit to harm. He grieves with you over what has been done to your heart, body, and soul.

But this is not the end of your story. The fact that you are reading this today shows your courage and desire for things to change. And God is invested in helping you do that.

What others have tried to break, God is able to restore. Your pain is real, your boundaries and feelings matter, and you don't have to minimize what has happened. Healing is possible and is within reach.

Prayer:

Dear Father, intimacy in my marriage has been distorted, leaving me confused and wounded. Help me to protect my body and my heart as I walk in Your truth. Help all that has been hidden in my marriage come to light. And help me to be wise and discerning in every step I take. Amen.

Action Steps:

At the back of this book, you'll find resources for pornography addiction for your healing and, if you choose to share them, for your husband, should he choose to seek help. Remember: It is not your responsibility to research or fix his struggles. Your focus will need to be on your healing, boundaries, and wholeness. Use these resources as tools to protect your heart, gain clarity, and walk forward in freedom, whether you choose to navigate this alone or alongside your spouse.

Note: If your husband has committed adultery or has solicited sex, prioritize your physical safety by seeking a professional for comprehensive STD testing. If your husband has been found viewing child pornography or molesting a child, I urge you to get to safety right away.

Day 12
Naming What's Hard to Name: Financial Abuse

"She is clothed with strength and dignity; she can laugh at the days to come. Her children arise and call her blessed; her husband also, and he praises her: honor her for all that her hands have done."

Proverbs 31:25, 28, 31

———Pause. Take a few deep breaths. Now rest—and abide in Him.———

We often hear about the Proverbs 31 woman in terms of how she honors her husband and cares for her family with diligence and nurturing care. But what we don't always talk about is the freedom she had. She was trusted by her husband with resources, autonomy, and financial responsibility. She was empowered to make decisions, to steward what was hers, and to contribute to the household with wisdom and confidence.

Sadly, not every marriage reflects this God-given partnership. What should be mutual respect and trust can turn into control, manipulation, and restriction. When dignity, independence, and the ability to participate fully in financial decisions are stripped away, financial abuse begins.

Financial abuse is not just about money—it's about power. It shows up when a spouse dictates what you can or can't spend, sabotages your job opportunities, limits access to resources, or keeps you dependent and constrained.

For years, I struggled with chronic inflammatory disorders that were worsened by stress. Managing my health with limited resources was a constant strain, especially when the things I needed, like vitamins or allergy-sensitive foods, were expensive.

I remember standing in line at the grocery store with my heart pounding, sweating as I counted the cash my husband had allotted me. I was over budget by about $20 and knew my husband would question why I had spent so much. I had been under so much stress at home that I cracked right there in the checkout aisle and began to sob.

A woman behind me noticed and offered to pay the difference. She wasn't the first, and she wouldn't be the last. Sometimes my allowance was bigger, or he was generous in ways that felt kind, but it was never consistent—I never knew when those times would come. The constant uncertainty and frequent scrutiny were exhausting.

Financial abuse takes an emotional toll. It traps you in fear and anxiety, erodes your confidence, and leaves you questioning your worth.

Your story may look different than mine. Maybe in your marriage, it shows up as reckless spending, plunging the family into debt, gambling, large purchases without consulting you, or never knowing if your husband will keep his job. Maybe your spouse is a very generous giver to others but ignores your needs all together.

Here's the truth: You are worthy of a life free from financial chaos. God made you an intelligent Proverbs 31 woman, capable of making decisions in your family's financial situation. You deserve financial peace, security, and respect. And if you are a stay-at-home mom, don't believe the lie that you shouldn't have any say-so in the finances because you don't earn the money. God created you and your husband to be partners.

Scripture makes God's heart clear on this: "But if anyone does not provide for his own, and especially for those of his household, he has denied the faith and is worse than an unbeliever" (1 Timothy 5:8, NKJV).

I want you to know: Your strength and resilience are more powerful than you realize. You can reclaim your life, with God's help, one step at a time.

Prayer:

Heavenly Father, I know You own the cattle on a thousand hills and that You are a generous and faithful Provider. But something has been off in my marriage, and I feel the strain and confusion around our finances. Please help me to see clearly what I'm experiencing and discern whether it reflects Your heart. Give me wisdom to take steps toward financial stability and freedom. Amen.

Reflection:

Take a moment and reflect on your family's finances and your role in them. Has your input been valued or dismissed? Do you feel a sense of stability and shared responsibility, or do you often feel anxious about your husband's spending, frequent job changes, or financial decisions? Have there been times when money was used to control, manipulate, or keep you dependent? Ask God to show you what financial peace and partnership should look like in your marriage.

Day 13
Naming What's Hard to Name: Spiritual Abuse

"He will not crush the weakest reed or put out a flickering candle. He will bring justice to all who have been wronged."

Isaiah 42:3, NLT

——*Pause. Take a few deep breaths. Now rest—and abide in Him.*——

The Bible is meant to comfort, exhort, uplift, and draw us closer to Christ. But when Scripture is twisted to control, punish, demean, or confuse us, it wounds instead of heals. Spiritual abuse can take many forms, twisting Scriptures to keep you in line, weaponizing prayer to make you feel guilty, using the Bible to harshly discipline your children, or even excusing abuse in God's name.

Maybe, for you, that looked like your husband praying verses over your "rebellious and selfish heart" when you set a boundary on *his* bad behavior—that's not godly leadership; that's spiritual manipulation and hypocrisy, which Jesus addressed frequently. Or maybe he sermonizes you with long speeches about what you *should* believe, insisting his version of faith is the only way. But here's the truth: high-control religion demands compliance rather than heart transformation, and that kind of pressure doesn't draw people toward Christ—it pushes them away. And this includes our children.

Maybe he used Scripture to dictate how you dress, eat, speak, or act. This is control, not holiness. Or maybe your spouse is out "winning souls," but at home, he treats you as if you don't matter—or worse. Or maybe it's the opposite—your husband mocks your faith, belittles your prayers, or even prevents you from going to church or being with other believers.

Other times, spiritual abuse happens in the very place that should feel like a refuge—your church. You may be met with shame, silence, or insinuations that separating from an abusive spouse shows a lack of faith. Maybe your church preaches that "submission" means obeying everything your husband says, even if it harms you or your children. But that is not the heart of God, who would never force His daughters into oppression.

I've known this pain personally. I never stopped believing in God, but for a time, I was physically revolted when I tried to do the things that had once brought me peace and joy. There was a season when I desperately wanted to worship with others but simply couldn't. My body would react with tears, sweats, and anxiety at even a hint of controlling or twisted teachings.

Reading my Bible sometimes stirred more pain than peace—and my prayers felt heavy and stale. I never doubted God—I loved Him deeply—but the things connected to Him had been so misused that, no matter how much my soul and mind longed to draw near, my nervous system would shut down. It took intentional, gentle effort to slowly convince my body that it was safe again to reconnect.

Just before I sat down to write this, I read Psalm chapter 37, which speaks of delighting in the Lord and trusting Him. While these words are a balm to my soul today, I realize for some they might not be. Maybe that's you.

If this is where you find yourself, please hear this: You are not sinful or faithless for feeling this way. You are responding in a very human way to things that are wrong and unjust.

Instead of suppressing these feelings, I want to encourage you to take them to God. Your words may be raw, messy, full of lament or even anger. That's OK. God is not afraid of your honesty. He has seen what you've endured, and He holds space for every emotion you're feeling, even mistrust. And if you can't even do that in this season—please hear me—just rest. God understands.

God is patient, kind, and understanding as we heal. He won't rush you, and He will never shame you. What others have done is not a reflection of who He is.

Don't allow anyone to take away your relationship with God. Cling to what you know to be true. He is a God of love and not force. He will never harm you or control you. Yes, He will continue to grow you and convict you of true sin, but He will never force you to do anything against your will. He loves you too much for that.

Prayer:

Dear God, please meet me where I am, confused, hurt, and unsure. Help me feel Your presence as being safe and trustworthy. Heal the places in me that have been wounded by the misuse of Your Word. Show me the truth and show me that I am loved by You. Amen.

Reflection:

Take time to reflect on your current relationship with God. Have there been times when His name or His Word felt unsafe because of how they were used? What parts of your faith feel tender or confusing right now. Don't hold back or filter yourself; just let your raw, honest feelings rise to the surface. God can handle your questions, confusion, pain, and even your anger. He longs to meet you right where you are.

Day 14

Naming What's Hard to Name: Betrayal Trauma

"I will lead the blind by ways they have not known, along unfamiliar paths I will guide them; I will turn the darkness into light before them and make the rough places smooth. These are the things I will do; I will not forsake them."

Isaiah 42:16

Have you suddenly found yourself thrust into detective mode because something doesn't feel quite right? One day, everything seems fine in your marriage—and then a heavy fog rolls in. It's like waking up to find your world shrouded in mist: Everything looks familiar, but nothing feels clear anymore. You can't see the path ahead, and every step feels uncertain. Suddenly, the life you once knew shifts into something unrecognizable.

Maybe it's a walk into the room late at night that reveals your husband staring at pornography. Or a phone call from "the other woman." Or a forced disclosure after years of sexual sin, escorts, and addiction. Betrayal. Trauma. Pain. Shame. And *absolute* disillusionment.

Betrayal trauma occurs when someone you depend on for safety, love, or support seriously violates your trust, causing your sense of security to collapse. It cuts to the deepest part of your soul.

It feels unfair, deceptive, and unsafe. Suddenly you don't even know who this man is that you've been sharing a bed with all these years. Your stomach twists in knots, and you don't know if you want to withdraw, cry, scream, or hurt him.

After discovering pornography use, infidelity, emotional affairs, or hidden sexual sin, you may experience a flood of distressing emotions—hypervigilance, loss of trust, or ruminating thoughts. You might feel uneasy or triggered by women who remind you of your husband's type, or feel insecure in ways that are new and unfamiliar. Have grace on yourself; this isn't your fault.

As you begin to heal, it's important to keep these three "C's" in mind:

1. You didn't cause this.
2. You can't cure it.
3. You can't control it.

Betrayal trauma naturally leads us to question ourselves: "Why am I not enough?" "What does she have that I don't?" It makes us question our reality: "How much of our life together has been a lie?" And it can leave us feeling like we may never be able to trust another human being, let alone our husband.

You may already be on the path to healing, or you may just be beginning. Think of the path to recovery in three parts: your recovery, his recovery, and—*if* you decide to stay—the work you do together. The first two need to happen first and separately. You need time to process and heal in a safe space. Remember, you are the one betrayed—you have permission not to extend trust blindly. When your husband breaks your trust at this level, it will need to be earned going forward.

According to Dr. Patrick Carnes, expert on sex addiction and treatment, there are phases you'll go through as you work toward healing: the discovery phase, the crisis phase, then shock, grief, and ambivalence. Then reaching the repair stage, where you focus on your self-care and needs, and finally, the stage described as growth, where you move from being a victim to becoming a survivor and overcomer.

If this is a part of your story, I want to encourage you, don't try to walk this alone. Betrayal trauma creates wounds and needs to be processed. But with support, prayer, and intentional steps toward reclaiming your identity and sense of safety, you can find healing.

Dear friend, this journey may be slow and rugged at times, but each step you take is a step toward healing. God truly can be trusted and wants to walk through the fog with you to help clear the path.

Prayer:

Dear God, I'm angry, sad, hurt, and confused. I don't understand why my husband has chosen to hurt me. The pain is deep, and I desperately need Your healing. Help me to be wise so I can protect my body and soul. Give me the strength to set boundaries as I watch for signs of true repentance or if I decide to leave, please be with me every step of the way. Amen.

Reflection:

What steps can you take to ensure your body, mind, and heart are safe as you work on healing? What consistent actions (not words) show you that your husband is truly repentant and working on rebuilding trust? If trust cannot be rebuilt, what kind of support and boundaries might help you move forward in truth and healing—even if that means releasing the relationship?

Note: If your husband is involved in child pornography or molestation, these warrant contacting the authorities, as well as immediate separation and beginning your healing from a safe distance. If your husband has been sexually active with other women, getting tested for sexually transmitted diseases is an essential and wise step to protect your health.

Day 15

Naming Undiagnosed Conditions & Untreated Addictions

*"The Lord is close to the brokenhearted and
saves those who are crushed in spirit."*

Psalm 34:18

———*Pause. Take a few deep breaths. Now rest—and abide in Him.*———

Dr. Jim Wilder describes two types of trauma that shape our emotional lives. According to his classifications, Trauma A is the "absence" of the good and necessary things that give us emotional stability. This type is often overlooked, but can be just as impactful as Trauma B, which refers to the overt "bad" things that happen to us, such as physical or sexual assault, among other things. Trauma A arises when we experience deep emotional neglect, rejection, or prolonged absence of care, leaving lasting wounds that may not be as obvious to others.

Many women find themselves in marriages where Trauma A is present. From the outside, the marriage may look fine, but on the inside, something is very wrong.

So let's talk about some things that can lead to Trauma A. First, if your husband is dealing with a neurodivergent disorder, a mental health condition, or unresolved trauma, it can profoundly affect you and your children. Second, if he is struggling with addiction, this can also often impact everyone around him.

Maybe you've started to sink into a deep sadness because your marriage feels like a constant struggle. You don't see your husband as "abusive," and the pain he causes doesn't seem intentional, yet his actions—or lack of emotional responsiveness—wound you deeply. You can't quite put your finger on what's wrong, but you know something clearly is.

He may drift through daily life disconnected, struggle to follow through on tasks, or seem oblivious to your emotional cues. When you speak up, he shuts down or lashes out and genuinely believes your reactions are the problem. You might notice patterns of excitability, mania, bluntness, or an inability to hold a conversation, or, at the other extreme, depression, flat affect, or withdrawal from the relationship.

He may react intensely to perceived criticisms, struggle to empathize, or cling to rigid routines, religious legalism, or perfectionism. Neurodivergence, unresolved trauma, mood disorders, or personality disorders can create a host of challenges within a marriage if not dealt with properly. Whatever the cause, the impact on you is real. Maybe you're holding together the household, the schedule, and the emotional weight of the relationship while he drifts through life unaware.

If your husband is undiagnosed—or diagnosed but unwilling to address his challenges—you need to assess the true impact on you and your children and take steps to safeguard your well-being.

Second, you may be navigating addictions. These may or may not be obvious, and they may or may not be caused by the things we just discussed, but often are. While drinking alcohol does not automatically make a marriage unsafe, excess use can. Addictions, such as drugs, alcohol, gambling, sexual acting out, or pornography, often lead to secrecy, lying, and instability and can leave you carrying practical and emotional burdens alone.

If your husband is willing to get help, change is possible. But, it's important to understand that it may take time to see change with some mental health conditions and disorders, or change may be very limited if your husband has challenges that truly affect his ability to function. Change might come from medications (for some conditions), therapy to process trauma, recovery programs for addiction, or counseling/coaching to manage neurodivergent behaviors. The key is his willingness to face his issues honestly, take responsibility, and actively work toward growth—because without it, the burden remains on you.

Remember, even when the struggle feels invisible to others, God isn't causing your pain, but He sees it and cares deeply about helping you find a way out of it. Dear friend, God is close. Psalm 34:18 says, "The Lord is close to the brokenhearted and saves those who are crushed in spirit." You don't have to carry all of this alone. When you start taking the steps to care for yourself and your children, God promises to walk with you, because He wants to lead you out of the fog and into the light.

Prayer:

Dear Heavenly Father, open my eyes to what is happening in my marriage, even the things that are hard to name. Give me the courage to have hard conversations, set boundaries where needed, and prioritize my emotional, physical, and spiritual well-being. Amen.

Reflection:

What patterns or behaviors have you noticed in your marriage that make you wonder if your husband might have a disorder, a mental health challenge, or an addiction? Has he been diagnosed, but is unwilling to seek help? What conversations do you need to have, and what boundaries do you need to set? If these challenges don't apply to your marriage, how is your own emotional well-being, and are there areas where you might need additional support?

Day 16
The Lie of Mutual Brokenness

"The Lord will fight for you; you need only to be still."
Exodus 14:14

———*Pause. Take a few deep breaths. Now rest—and abide in Him.*———

Dear friend, if you're here reading this today, I imagine you are an honest, deeply committed woman. One who has prayed, tried, waited, and worked yourself to near exhaustion trying to hold your marriage together. Maybe you've spent years asking yourself, "What more can I do?" Or you're now to the point of asking, "How do I stay sane, whether or not my marriage survives?"

I want to honor that part of you that has already given so much. Maybe you've looked at your own heart, your childhood wounds, your triggers, your perfectionism, and your patterns. You've listened when your husband said you're nagging, not submitting enough, or not respecting him. So, you looked inside again and again, taking stock and trying harder.

You've gone the extra mile to make sure your "side of the street" is clean. In fact, many women I work with have swept their side of the street so often and so thoroughly that their broom handles are about to break off! And yet, despite all your effort, your husband's harmful behaviors persist, and his side of the street is left littered with messes.

Maybe you've sat in couples counseling, only to be told again that there's one more thing *you* could try to make your marriage work—be gentler, more forgiving, or more patient when he raises his voice.

I even remember being "counseled" once to think of my husband's yelling and screaming like a wind tunnel—and to just sit through it so he could fully express himself.

But deep down, you know that no matter how much you give, the best you can hope for in return is the bare minimum of human decency—if he changes at all.

Dear one, this is where we need to let the lie die. Abuse is not a "couple's issue." Nor is it an issue of mutual brokenness to be solved with a 50/50 approach. Abuse *creates* the issues. Abuse is one person's choice to harm, control, or demean another. It isn't something that can be remedied by you being a better wife, housekeeper, lover, or peacekeeper.

When destructive patterns, such as emotional abuse, adultery, pornography, or infidelity are present, the responsibility for change lies with the one who is causing the damage. Period. Until that person takes ownership of their actions and demonstrates true repentance through their words and actions, over an extended period of time, the relationship cannot and will not heal.

This is why traditional couples counseling, marriage retreats, or untrained pastoral counseling often does more harm than good for unsafe and unsustainable marriages, and can even further traumatize you.

Instead, you will need to adopt a new way of approaching things—with a radical commitment to reality. Name what is happening: Emotional abuse. Betrayal. Addiction. Control. Then, and only then, can the work of healing begin. First for you, as you work to restore safety and stability, and then, possibly, for your spouse and the marriage. But that will be up to him. He alone must make the choice to get help and pursue healing and recovery.

Friend, please remember this: God never asks any of us to sacrifice ourselves for someone else's sin. He invites us to walk in truth—and freedom. He sees the years you've spent trying to save your marriage, and He is whispering to your heart today: "You have done enough. You can rest now."

Is it time you rest in the One who sees and loves you, instead of trying to do more for the one who isn't honoring your efforts? If so, lean into the arms of Jesus today and allow your wearied and busy heart to rest.

Prayer:

Dear Heavenly Father, I am weary and worn from years of trying to fix my marriage. You have seen my efforts and know my heart. Please help me to see the truth clearly and to be honest about the state of my husband's heart and his willingness to change. Teach me how to tend my side of the street in a different way: to focus on my boundaries and the work You need me to do to heal. Remind me that I don't have to carry what isn't mine to carry. Help me rest in Your care while I release my husband and my marriage to You. Amen.

Reflection:

Write down some of the ways you've worked to keep your marriage healthy—emotionally, spiritually, practically. How have these efforts been received or reciprocated? What do his responses reveal about his willingness—or unwillingness—to change?

Be honest with yourself: Have you been overfunctioning or enabling in the hopes of receiving love that never comes? As you do this, be sure to have compassion for yourself. Seeing the truth clearly after deep pain or betrayal can be both freeing and hard at the same time.

To learn more about why couples counseling is not recommended when there's been abuse, visit: www.darahashlie.com/blog/no-couples-counseling-abuse

Day 17
God Does Not Use Abuse to Sanctify

"But God disciplines us for our good."
Hebrews 12:10

——*Pause. Take a few deep breaths. Now rest—and abide in Him.*——

Without even realizing it, many of us view God through the lens of our earthly fathers. Some of us grew up with fathers who mirrored God's love and protection in beautiful ways. And others had fathers who were the exact opposite—not true reflections of our Father in heaven. That's why Hebrews 12:9 can feel complicated for some:

> We have *all* had human fathers who disciplined us, and we respected them for it. How much more should we submit to the Father of spirits and live! They disciplined us for a little while as they thought best; but God disciplines us for our good, in order that we may share in his holiness (emphasis added).

But what if your earthly father didn't discipline you out of love? What if he was overly controlling, harsh, neglectful, or even abusive? The same can be true for your mother or another caregiver—sometimes the very adults meant to protect us wound us deeply instead.

These early experiences can shape how we see authority, care, and protection in all of our relationships, even in our marriage. If you grew up in a home with a father who didn't follow God—or worse, one who let the enemy use him to harm you—it can be difficult to see God as a loving Father with your best interests at heart. Having a clear vision of who God is and His corrections may feel confusing.

Christian circles add to this confusion by saying things like, "Marriage is to make us holier, not happier." For those of us who have lived through cycles of pain and dysfunction in our marriage, this is a deeply destructive teaching. And, if you grew up with harmful family dynamics, this could sink even heavier in your heart, because you may already have some of these misbeliefs about the nature of God hidden in the crevices of your heart.

Here's the truth: God *does* care about our happiness. And God is not like the broken human examples we may have known. He's not a hurtful father, or an unsafe, unfaithful, neglectful, or overly controlling spouse. And no matter what anyone has said, God would never intentionally use abuse or dysfunction from a spouse to try to make you holier. He didn't create marriage to be a crucible that you're just meant to endure so your character can be "perfected." His nature isn't like that. And His discipline and the means He uses to grow our characters flow from perfect love and wisdom, never pride, selfishness, or cruelty.

He does not use abuse to sanctify anyone. Because abuse does not lead to holiness—it leads to shattered lives. God's correction is meant to restore, protect, guide, and grow us.

Abusive marriages do not make anyone holier—they destroy people. God would never use a controlling, harsh, or abusive spouse to correct you or try to "reach" you. That is just *not* His nature.

Yet there is hope. God's heart is full of love for you, and He longs to protect and restore you. He wants to be a Father to you like no one on Earth ever could be—even if you had a wonderful father. He sees every wound, every tear, and every moment of pain you've endured. And He invites you into His care. Take His hand, and allow Him to lead you toward safety, healing, and peace.

His love will never harm you, and His guidance will always be for your good.

Prayer:

Dear God, help me to see You as You truly are: loving, kind, peaceful; not vengeful, yet full of healthy mercy and justice. Please heal the wounds left by my earthly father (or mother), my husband, or both. Lord, help me today to start fresh in my relationship with You, as I continue to walk in truth. Amen.

Reflection:

Write down your feelings about God. Have you seen Him as angry, distant, or vengeful, or felt He hasn't protected you? Reflect on where these feelings may have come from. Are they connected to the lack of love seen by one or both parents, or from your husband? Be honest with yourself and give the younger you the grace and compassion you needed then. Allow yourself to explore these connections without judgment.

Day 18
You Are Not a Rebellious Woman

"Behold, I send you out as sheep in the midst of wolves. Therefore, be wise as serpents and harmless as doves."
Matthew 10:16, NKJV

———*Pause. Take a few deep breaths. Now rest—and abide in Him.*———

You are not a rebellious woman for not wanting to submit to someone who repeatedly harms you or your children or has hidden dark and disturbing secrets for years. You are not a rebellious woman for wanting justice or for stepping away from patterns of sin and destruction, even if your church or family tells you that you are. You are acting wisely, not disobediently.

Let me tell you about another wise woman from the Bible. Her name was Tamar.

Tamar was married to a man named Er, but according to the Bible, Er was a wicked man, so "the Lord killed him" (Genesis 38:7). According to the custom of that time, her father-in-law, Judah, had another son, Onan, who was supposed to marry Tamar so she could bear children and continue the family line. But Onan sinned against Tamar by refusing her children, which displeased God, and God put him to death as well (Genesis 38:10).

Judah then promised that when his youngest son, Shelah, came of age, he would give him in marriage to Tamar. However, when that time came, he knowingly broke his promise. And Tamar was left vulnerable and without protection or provision. As we can see, dysfunction has a way of running in some families (but that's a devotional for another day!).

Now, Tamar could have silently submitted to Judah's wrongdoing. But she didn't. She discerned right from wrong and took a bold step. She disguised herself, and while Judah was unaware of who she was, he slept with her. Tamar became pregnant with twins, thus giving her the rightful inheritance and security she had been denied.

Once Judah discovered Tamar was pregnant, he called for her to be punished. But when Tamar revealed that he was the father, Judah declared, "She is more righteous than I, since I would not give her to my son" (Genesis 38:26).

To some, Tamar's actions might look rebellious, maybe even scandalous. But not to God.

God honored Tamar's unwillingness to condone sin and stay silent with this family's dysfunction. In Scripture, Tamar isn't remembered with shame but with honor. Generations later, in the book of Ruth, we see her story mentioned as a blessing: "May your family be like that of Perez, whom Tamar bore to Judah" (Ruth 4:12). And because of her actions, Tamar is in the lineage of Jesus Himself (Matthew 1:3).

Dear friend, God never asks us to quietly endure sin against us or our children. Too often, the church confuses the call to suffer for Christ with suffering for a spouse's sin. But they are not the same.

God calls us to wisdom, discernment, and courage in the face of wrongdoing. Just as He honored Tamar for not enabling sin, He honors your steps to stand against sin in your marriage and to protect yourself and your children.

You are not rebellious for seeking healing and safety. You can love your husband without loving his sin. And you are not disobedient for refusing to submit to abuse. You are walking the very hard path of being "wise as a serpent, yet gentle as a dove," and God honors this (Matthew 10:16).

Know that God is with you today. God never tires of being your protector. He sees your vigilance, your courage, and your pain. He promises to be your refuge and your strength, and ever-present help in trouble (Psalm 46:1).

Prayer:

Dear Heavenly Father, protect me and my children. Help me not to condone sin and not allow it to continue harming us. Help me as I continue this new journey to learn how I can grow stronger and more courageous like Tamar. And help me to stay gentle as a dove, yet be wise as a serpent to protect my heart and my children's hearts. Amen.

Reflection:

Have you been labeled or made to feel "rebellious" when you've pointed out your husband's sin? Have you internalized that belief? Reflect on Tamar's story—how did her courage and discernment honor God? How does her story speak into your own story and your desire to protect your children and your heart?

Day 19
Settling for Scraps of Affection

*"Blessed is the one who does not walk in step with
the wicked or stand in the way that sinners take or
sit in the company of mockers."*

Psalm 1:1

———*Pause. Take a few deep breaths. Now rest—and abide in Him.*———

Let's talk about "settling" for a moment. I spent what felt like a lifetime settling.

I settled as a teen, because I hurt. Pain had taught me to accept whatever scraps of affection others would give me. That didn't end well.

I settled as I grew older, because I thought, *I am getting older, so I have to settle in my relationships, in my circumstances.* That was a lie, too.

I settled because I was never told I was good enough. I wasn't told God had better for me. And deep down, I didn't feel I was worthy of better. I settled because pain and past trauma had taught me lessons that spoke shame and unworthiness deep into the fabric of my soul.

I even settled at times because I felt sorry for someone else or pitied them, so I allowed them a spot in my inner world. But their presence took away my energy and strength for healthy others that God had intended to fill their place.

Sometimes we settle for relationships that are not healthy because we're lonely or because we're operating out of a place of desperation. Or even because we believe that God would surely want us to "love" everybody. And He does. But He doesn't call us to be in close fellowship, inner friendship, or intimacy with just anybody. He wants us as Christian women to fill our inner circle with the best—because settling is a truly *unsettling* place to be.

When we settle for less than God's best in our lives and in our relationships, pain often follows.

Please hear me, sweet friend: If you're a woman who has been settling in life because you feel like you have to—you don't.

You don't have to settle for less in your career, in your dreams for the future, in your living situation, in your friendships, and especially not in your marriage. Will any of these things ever be perfect? No, not this side of heaven. But they shouldn't be destructive, unsafe, or abusive.

And while I do believe that we're called to a level of contentment in all things, settling is quite different. While God's peace is available to us no matter our lot and we're called to love people, that doesn't mean we should operate from a place of desperation. God is not calling us to accept just anything or anybody into our lives, especially into the nearest and dearest places in our lives.

You don't have to accept scraps of affection from others. God doesn't expect you to.

God wants us to operate from a place of our true worth, from a place of principles, and from a place of discernment. It's OK to wait for God's best. Don't let loneliness or lack of worth push you into things you know are not part of God's plan for your life.

In Psalm 1:1 (KJV), God tells us this: "Blessed is the one who walks not in the counsel of the ungodly, nor stands in the path of sinners, nor sits in the seat of the scornful."

God is saying don't allow yourself to be influenced by a fool or by anyone who doesn't treat you as God's precious daughter. You don't have to stay in fellowship with someone if they keep sinning against you. Because God doesn't want *you* being changed by their scornful attitudes and behaviors. God is saying choose who you allow into your inner circle wisely.

Don't just settle or accept when others choose you—or even force themselves into your life.

God has a plan and a purpose for your future, and it includes the best things; don't settle for less.

Prayer:

Dear Father, I have allowed the pain in my life to whisper lies to me. To make me believe I am not worthy of true, respectful love and friendship. Please give me discernment to recognize what in my relationships is unhealthy and guide me in the steps I need to take to protect my heart and walk in Your truth.

Reflection:

Where have you been settling in your life—your marriage, friendships, church, or personal goals? What patterns or unhealthy compromises have you accepted that make you feel depleted, unvalued, or overlooked? How might God be inviting you to seek for His best instead of accepting less?

Day 20
A Deeper Kind of Lonely

"Husbands, love your wives and never treat them harshly."
Colossians 3:19, NLT

———*Pause. Take a few deep breaths. Now rest—and abide in Him.*———

There is a loneliness that is deeper than being alone. It's the loneliness of being with someone who deeply neglects you. If you're married to a spouse who refuses to invest in your life in any way, who continually makes you feel silly for your hobbies, or who mocks your desires, likes, and dislikes, your marriage isn't healthy.

Often, we stay in harmful and unsafe relationships because we fear the alternative. It can feel scary to imagine being alone after being with someone. Or we stay because being a wife is what we always felt called to be, or because we hold out hope that our husband will change.

I feel certain you didn't commit yourself in marriage with the thought that it would ever end. I didn't. It can feel like the death of a dream. And yet if your marriage has shifted from dream to nightmare, it's vital you don't let your fear become louder than your discernment.

We aren't in an emotionally safe place when we fear the unknown so much that we're willing to accept dysfunction in place of true, Christ-like love. God designed marriage to be a place where both partners attune to one another. The divide should not become so deep and wide that one partner feels starved for any shred of attention or affection.

But I've seen the pattern over and over again. An unfaithful husband allows his wife to wither from affection. An addicted husband sets aside the feelings of his wife because he can only attune to the thing he is addicted to, whether that's pornography, alcohol, or any other addiction. And then there's the emotionally unavailable or unregulated husband who draws near to his wife only when he wants sex, otherwise he steps on her heart, belittles her, controls her, gaslights her, or ignores her completely.

You are worth far more than fragments. You are worthy of being loved by your spouse in ways that are protective, safe, and respectful. You are worthy of being with someone who would never continue to harm you, knowingly or "unknowingly," as some abusive partners will claim. It's true that sometimes our spouse can unintentionally hurt us, but when the same behaviors become patterns, they're no longer accidents—they're choices.

Sweet friend, you were not created to wither from neglect or to be starved of true love and affection. God made you for so much more. And God made marriage for so much more. He created it to be a place of safety—of being seen. And while only God can love us in a perfect way, it's not too much to expect that your spouse loves you with tenderness, care, and respect.

You're allowed to ask for more, to want more, and when it's needed, to set firm boundaries that protect your soul. That is not rebellion—it's wisdom, and it honors the God who calls you beloved and made you for so much more.

Prayer:

Jesus, thank You for seeing me for who I truly am. That I am known by You. And that You never neglect me. Help me to rest in the knowledge that You created me for the kind of love that respects and honors who I was created to be. Teach me to walk in Your wisdom and not in my fear, and to know when to extend grace and when to set boundaries to protect the heart You have entrusted to me. Amen.

Reflection:

What does God's love look like toward you, and how does that differ from how you are being treated in your marriage? What is one small boundary you could set to reclaim your worth today?

Day 21

Damsel, Arise! It's Time to Care for Your Life

"And he took the damsel by the hand, and said unto her, 'Talitha cumi; which is, being interpreted, 'Damsel, I say unto thee, arise.'"
Mark 5:41, KJV

——*Pause. Take a few deep breaths. Now rest—and abide in Him.*——

In Mark 5, there is a story of a damsel everyone believed to be dead. There was crying and weeping over her as Jesus approached. He corrected the scene by telling them she was not dead but simply sleeping. While they laughed at Him, He put away the scorners, closed the door, and gently called, "Damsel, arise." He knew He was able to call her to life—and that, in fact, she would rise.

You may feel like that damsel—on the brink of spiritual death, emotional death, maybe even physical death. Abuse of any kind, betrayal of the closest kind, or the sheer exhaustion of navigating a spouse's addictions can leave your faith flickering, your mind ill or depressed, and your body at the edge of collapse.

And all of these things are likely not just feelings. They hold truth. When our souls experience dis-ease, our minds and bodies follow suit. Dis-ease can become disease. Trauma reshapes our minds—it can lead to chronic overwhelm, anxiety, depression, PTSD, or CPTSD. And trauma lives in our bodies.

Many abused women end up becoming regulars at the doctor's office, with one unexplained condition after another. Sometimes abuse and betrayal lead to years of stress that settle into our stomachs, our joints, our backs—rooted deep within our bodies.

But, sweet friend, none of this is beyond hope. While trauma is real and its effects are real—and cannot not be minimized or "spiritualized away"—with intentional time and effort healing can begin, even if some pieces of our story remain with us. God is powerful to heal.

Our minds have neuroplasticity, which means that as you begin to heal from the abuse or stress of the betrayal, your mind can adapt and take on new, healthy thoughts and patterns. Old neural pathways that lead to triggering thoughts, maladaptive coping mechanisms, and destructive self-beliefs can die off as you prioritize new healthy routines. The brain favors usage.

And your body can heal, too; God created it that way. But both take intentional effort. First, by lessening the time you're exposed to stress and chaos by setting boundaries. (Don't worry, we will talk more about this soon.)

Second, by making your care—and your children's care—a priority. Self-care is vital, not selfish.

Ask yourself: What am I feeding myself, how am I resting myself, how am I moving myself—and am I being tender with myself? Training yourself to breathe deeply and intentionally is part of healing your nervous system. Gentle, soothing movement can help restore the body's balance after trauma. And remembering what you focus on shapes your mental well-being. These small, yet sacred acts become the scaffolding of your restoration.

Guard your time as you heal. Now is not the time to take on ten new projects or five new clubs for the kiddos. This may be the season to slim down—to focus on what truly nourishes you, not what drains you. This includes finding safe people who feed your soul.

Maybe you feel like you're standing at death's door—maybe metaphorically, maybe even literally. But Jesus sees you. He knows this is not your end, but a season.

Dear friend, God is in the business of raising the dead to life. Where you once experienced pain and destruction, allow Him to revive what's been lost. You can do this. Take the one next step He shows you toward healing your mind, body, and soul.

Prayer:

Dear Heavenly Father, thank You for giving me a mind and body that can heal. Help me to trust that if there are lingering effects or illnesses in my mind or body that You will be with me to comfort and guide me. Please help me to take my health and care seriously. Help me to see that as I model self-care, I'm teaching my children to do the same. Help me to know the next right step, and show me which areas of my mind, body, and soul need my attention. Amen.

Reflection:

What steps is God asking you to take to better care for yourself? What do you need to tend to for your mind? For your body? Are your relationships nourishing you or wearing you down? Are there things you need to take off your plate so you can focus on your and your children's self-care and healing? Or are there things you could add into your routine to be more present and to experience more joy?

Note: If you are being threatened or physically harmed, please turn to the Safety Plan link at the back of this devotional and fill it out. You deserve to be safe.

Day 22

Reading the Room

"For God has not given us a spirit of fear, but of power and of love and of a sound mind."

2 Timothy 1:7, NKJV

——*Pause. Take a few deep breaths. Now rest—and abide in Him.*——

Have you ever walked into the room and suddenly found yourself scanning your environment for signs of tension? Or looking for signs of uneasiness in your partner or any sign that they seem stressed or bothered?

You seem to notice their mood without them ever saying a word. You've become like a thermometer for their internal weather storms. Your body is like a detective trying to decipher every look, every sigh, every footstep. It causes you to guess and second guess endlessly, as you try to preserve calm and safety.

For those of us who have experienced an unsafe or unsustainable relationship, this can become a daily occurrence. We learn to "read the room" so we can avoid the next outburst, silent treatment used as punishment, or another sermon about what we've done wrong.

We learn that if we can make ourselves smaller, less of a target, or avoid interactions all together, we can avoid conflict. Over time our hyper-vigilance becomes our nervous system's new normal. The tension lives in the pit of our stomachs, in the stiffness of our necks, or in the beating of our overactive hearts—and it's exhausting. While this hyper-vigilance does serve a purpose for real threats, we don't want it taking over our nervous system in other situations when we are safe.

This isn't God's best for us. This is man's attempt at silencing us. God calls us to live in the peace He offers, not in the fear of what someone might do to us.

God never intended us to live in fear of the very person who is supposed to love, honor, and cherish us. His Word tells us His love is perfect and drives out all fear. It never leaves us second guessing our safety or sanity.

God wants to gently retrain our system and our hearts. To expect peace, not harm. To expect love, not hate. To learn to trust again, but with those who are safe. He wants us to be able to walk into a room without feeling a sense of dread. But this starts by putting ourselves in safe places where we aren't in harm's way. It starts with safe boundaries (more on this later), with speaking our truth in Christ-like ways, and with understanding we are worthy of peace.

God desires for us to learn to trust in our discernment again and not just in our fear. And He longs for us to know the safety of His heart, and not the confusion of our own.

Prayer:

Dear God, help me to begin to discern the times when I need to be vigilant for my safety and the times when I can rest. Help my nervous system to heal and help my mind to become clear so I can respond in wise ways. Amen.

Reflection/Action Step:

Begin to notice when you are "reading the room." Log in your journal after this happens and note the circumstances. When you find yourself doing it again, practice taking a pause, and take several deep cleansing breaths (or use your box breathing). Ask God to help you see the situation through His eyes. These steps can help slow down the nervous system and invite God's presence, allowing you to respond with wisdom.

* Remember, in times of actual threat, your nervous system is doing its job. Because in those times hyper-vigilance is protective and necessary. God wired us this way to keep us safe. The goal of this practice is not to suppress that instinct, but to help you return to a calmer, grounded state once safety is restored—and to think more clearly even when danger is present.

Day 23
External Vs. Internal Validation

"If any of you lacks wisdom, let him ask of God, who gives to all liberally and without reproach, and it will be given to him."

James 1:5, NKJV

———*Pause. Take a few deep breaths. Now rest—and abide in Him.*———

I have this one friend who holds a sacred spot in my heart. This friend walked with me through the darkest moments of my marriage. She was my sounding board, the one I could trust to tell me the truth when I tried to lie to myself.

"Oh, it's not that bad."

Or "He doesn't mean to hurt us."

"Nope," she'd say—compassionate, but firm. When wrong was wrong, she wouldn't sugar coat it. "Darah! That is just *so* wrong—he shouldn't be treating you two like this!" Then she'd usually end with an indignant little "grrrr."

She carried the strength I didn't have in those days. I didn't think I was even *allowed* to be upset. It never went well in my relationship if I expressed concern or frustration. And we were missionaries, after all. Didn't we have a "standard" to uphold?

Wasn't it *unChristian* to feel angry? To call something unjust? I had so much to untangle back then!

But my friend loved the Lord deeply, and because of that, I trusted her. Her righteous anger gave me permission to feel mine. She modeled what I couldn't yet grasp: Being a Christian doesn't mean staying silent in the face of abuse or dysfunction.

I desperately needed someone to validate my reality when I couldn't. I didn't have the bandwidth, courage, or clarity to do it on my own. And that's something many women in unsafe or unsustainable marriages struggle with.

When your reality has been denied, dismissed, or disputed long enough, you start to wonder if you can even trust your own thoughts. You've been told you're wrong for so long that trusting yourself feels scary.

So, you seek external validation and trust others to interpret your life for you, because their perspective feels more believable than your own. Your voice has been muted for so long, it feels safer to borrow someone else's.

But, sweet friend, healing comes when you start to reclaim your God-given voice. You were made in the image of God, with a mind and heart uniquely yours. And that same God, who knit you together in your mother's womb, is calling you to trust what He has placed inside of you. His still, small voice lives within you. You can discern truth. God promises that when we pray for wisdom, He is faithful to give it to us—we can trust this.

My friend and I still carry one another's burdens. But now, I've learned something she always knew: I can also trust my own perceptions. They were never the problem—someone else's misuse of power was.

Seek out those fierce, truth-loving friends who get what you're going through—especially those who love you enough to speak truth about the reality you are living in. But also, trust your own intuition. And allow God to restore the voice He gave you and let His truth rise within you.

Prayer:

Dear Heavenly Father, my trust has been broken in myself. I've been told for so long that I'm too much, too wrong, or that my opinion doesn't matter. I need Your help to believe in myself again. I need to be able to move forward without second-guessing everything. Please help me to trust that I am wise enough to discern right from wrong and continue to send me Your wisdom. Amen.

Reflection:

Who are your truth-telling friends? And if you can't think of any, is God calling you to find someone you can trust? Have you silenced yourself to keep the peace? What lies have you believed because you've been told them often enough, you accept them as truth?

Investing in Stability & Self-Care

The Transformation Phase

This is often a quiet season of transformation. In this season you'll be investing in your stability and self-care. If you have children, you'll help them to do this as well. From the outside, this season may look uneventful, but much like the unseen changes inside the cocoon, deep change is happening within you.

Here, you'll begin building rhythms that help your body, mind, and soul to heal. You'll begin to discover the beauty of rest, how to be more present, and how even small acts of self-care can help stabilize your life. These steps, much like the work the butterfly's body undergoes in this phase, are setting the stage for the strength you need going forward.

Lean into this hidden work. And allow God to rewire and untangle old survival habits and to steady your soul. It may feel slow or unseen, but it is holy and essential work. This is where you begin to discover that transformation is not about rushing forward but about being made whole from the inside out.

Day 24
From Chaos to Clarity

*"Peace I leave with you; my peace I give you. I do not give
to you as the world gives. Do not let your hearts be troubled
and do not be afraid."*

John 14:27

——Pause. Take a few deep breaths. Now rest—and abide in Him.——

What is true peace? It's the ability to walk through a heaving and chaotic world while feeling calm within. It's being in a situation with no clear path forward and still being able to sit in the uncertainty without being consumed by fear.

For many of us, the chaos has come in the form of cutting words, manipulation, neglect, or devastating secrets from the person who promised to love us. It's confusing and heart breaking. Yet, God's peace can meet us even in this.

Peace doesn't come from the absence of storms—it comes from abiding in the One who has authority over them. Jesus promised: "My peace I give you. I do not give to you as the world gives" (John 14:27). In Him is where we find clarity and calm.

Corrie Ten Boom, a woman who was sentenced to the concentration camps for hiding Jews during World War II, understood pain—maybe more than most ever will. She once described peace with an image of a little bird depicted in a painting she saw. The little bird rested quietly on a branch overhanging the mighty, roaring Niagara Falls, safe and still under its Creator's protection despite the raging waters that thundered beneath it. That is the kind of peace God is offering us.

The world often tells us to just get over our pain or gives us shallow reassurances or platitudes that everything will be fine. But true peace is different. It's knowing that even if everything is going wrong, we are being held by the One who can make it eternally and internally right—no matter what's happening around us. And with this peace as our anchor, we can step into the clarity God is ready to provide.

We can better understand that joy and sorrow can sit together. Chaos can swirl around us and calm still abide in us. Having peace doesn't mean our mess or even our anxiety suddenly disappears but it does mean we can trust the One who has overcome our mess.

I know how tempting it can be to think that peace will only come once your marriage is picture-perfect or your spouse finally changes. When the arguing stops, apologies are made, or your marriage is "fixed." But sometimes these things don't happen, or they only happen in part.

True peace is not dependent on another person's choices. It comes from knowing the One who holds you in His arms, even when the promises in your marriage have been broken. His peace allows us to step away from the confusion and into His clarity, even if the storms of life are still raging.

Prayer:

Dear God, my heart has been broken, and my peace has been stolen. Please restore both. I want to trust that even if I don't have all the answers, You are guiding me and covering me with Your protection. Help me to release what I can't control, to rest in Your presence, and to have compassion on myself when fear and worry still arise—because You do. Amen.

Reflection:

How might God be inviting you into His peace in this season, even amid uncertainty and fear? In what ways can you lean on Him to release your need for certain outcomes and open your heart to the clarity He may be offering for your situation and marriage?

Day 25
Calm Under the Storm

"He calms the storm, so that its waves are still. Then they are glad because they are quiet; so He guides them to their desired haven."
Psalm 107:29-30, NKJV

——*Pause. Take a few deep breaths. Now rest—and abide in Him.*——

My son and I loved to watch nature documentaries when he was growing up. I remember one in particular called *Secret Treasures of the Hidden Lakes*. It was about the rich underwater life found at the base of the Alps where lakes and rivers have formed from the cold mountain snow run-off.

In one of the scenes a scuba diver was exploring a cavernous lake with crystal clear blue waters. He looked as though he was suspended in thin air, trapped in a bubble of quiet beauty. Everything was pristine. Clear, clean, motionless, at peace.

It got me thinking about times when I've gone snorkeling. My son and I aren't avid snorkelers by any means but have been able to see some amazing spots around the world, from Papua New Guinea, the Philippines, Puerto Rico, the Caribbean, and along the coast of the US.

Each time we've been blessed to dive under God's blue waters, it's a reminder of how it can be in our life. On the surface of the water the waves are boisterous, even choppy and disturbing, but once you place your eyes and ears under the water's surface, you enter an entirely different world.

Diving down, you enter into peaceful nooks and crannies where whole ecosystems of life flourish that you never would have seen or known existed from above. There is an enveloping peace that sweeps over your surroundings as the sounds of crashing waves cease and the deafening silence of the water encircles you. It is true peace. I couldn't describe it any other way.

"There are depths in the ocean, which no tempest ever stirs—beyond the reach of all storms that sweep and agitate the surface of the sea" (LB Cowman, *Streams in the Desert*).

This is what God desires for our lives. He desires to draw us away from the crashing waves of life, the chaos and dysfunction, and usher us into a secret world of quiet and calm where He is ready to meet us with beauty unspeakable.

Dear friend, if you find your world rolling and heaving, don't let it take you away from having inner peace—remember that you have an anchor in Jesus, and He will hold you steady.

Prayer:

Dear Heavenly Father, despite the chaos in my life, help me to find the deep level of peace You are leading me into. Help me to trust that You will be my shelter in the storm. Amen.

Action Step:

Close your eyes and imagine diving deep beneath the stormy waves into the quiet, still blue waters beneath. Place one hand on your stomach and one hand over your heart, then take a deep breath in and exhale with the words: "Lord, calm my storm within." Use this whenever you're feeling overwhelmed and let it be your sacred space of peace.

Day 26

Celebrating the Small Wins

*"Do not despise these small beginnings,
for the Lord rejoices to see the work begin."*
Zechariah 4:10

———*Pause. Take a few deep breaths. Now rest—and abide in Him.*———

In life, we often look for the big moments—the milestones that feel "worth" celebrating. But the truth is, without the smaller steps, we would never build the strength or courage for the larger ones. Often, God entrusts us with "more" after we've been faithful in the little things first (Luke 16:10). This is why those seemingly insignificant moments matter so deeply.

What may look like just a drop in a vast ocean, in God's hands, can send out ripples farther than we ever imagined possible. Scripture speaks about these baby steps, "Do not despise these small beginnings, for the Lord rejoices to see the work begin" (Zechariah 4:10).

The first boundary you set may feel scary, but God knows it carries the seed of strength to say no again when it really matters. The first step toward clarity may feel uncertain, but could open the path to freedom. And that baby step of reclaiming your voice could lead to restoring your full identity in Him.

And something I feel I should add here about these small steps is this: They are much easier to take when someone is cheering us on.

I was reminded of this one morning when my dog, Scout, came to my bedside with a ball in his mouth, ready to play fetch. I, on the other hand, was more ready to roll over and go back to sleep. But I obliged.

Each time I threw it, I cheered him on to fetch it and bring it back—that seemed to be the key to actually getting the ball returned! After a few more throws, I stopped and began reading a devotional. But minutes later, I noticed Scout standing nearby, looking dejected. I could see it: He was about to give up. His head drooped and the ball dropped from his mouth. Mom wasn't interested or encouraging him anymore, so there was no reason in his little doggy heart to keep trying.

We're the same way. Encouragement keeps us moving. Lack of it can make us "drop the ball" entirely.

This is why safe people are so vital—women who can walk with you, cheer for you, and remind you that you're not alone on this path to healing. And if you can't think of anyone just yet, I'll be here encouraging you to celebrate and honor your victories along the way.

We often give up on our "big picture" goals when we don't honor the small steps it takes to get there. So, each devotional moving forward will end with this one final question: "What's one small step in your healing you can celebrate today?" Truly give this some thought, write it down in a journal or thank God in prayer for your wins. Do something that cements your progress in your mind. Because each step is evidence of movement. And progress begets progress.

A brave boundary. A moment you protected your peace. A decision not to return to what God has freed you from. A small act of parenting well in the middle of stress. A truth finally admitted to yourself.

We're not here seeking perfection—we're here seeking progress and healing. You don't have to have it all together. Just pause—breathe—and honor the one next step you're taking.

As much as we may wish healing would happen quickly, it takes time. So don't overlook the seemingly insignificant moments along the way—celebrate them. Mark them as new beginnings filled with possibility, because every step is evidence you're moving toward wholeness. Remember: God is not looking for *our ideal* of perfection but for our faithful progress.

I'm cheering you on, sweet friend. And, more importantly, your Heavenly Father is, too.

Prayer:

Dear God, thank You for the small changes that are leading me to make big changes. Changes that will have a ripple effect throughout the rest of my life and possibly the lives of those who depend on me. Help me to celebrate each step along the way, knowing it helps me to move toward the brighter future You have waiting for me. Amen.

Reflection:

I encourage you to keep a journal—or, if that feels like too much right now, at least a mental log—of your small steps. (If you do journal, it's wise to keep it tucked away privately.) One day, you'll be able to look back and see how those small steps formed the path God laid out as He walked with you toward freedom and healing. So, today, no matter how small your step toward healing, what is one win you can celebrate?

Day 27
Hooked on False Hope

"Hope deferred makes the heart sick, but a longing fulfilled is a tree of life."

Proverbs 13:12

———*Pause. Take a few deep breaths. Now rest—and abide in Him.*———

Have you ever seen an animal struggling for life, tangled and unable to free itself? I have. It was painful to watch—even if you're not especially fond of fish. Some may disagree, but any life fading is hard to witness, because deep down, we know this isn't how it's supposed to be.

One day, my son was exploring the lake near my parents' home and noticed a buoy bobbing strangely in the water. It jerked in small, random movements as if something unseen was tugging on it. Curious, he paddled over, pulled on the line, and found a three-foot-long catfish, stuck on a hook struggling beneath.

The fish was thoroughly worn out and looked as though he was near to death. Who knows how long he'd been dragging that buoy? My son brought him back to the dock, where he carefully removed the hook from his mouth and let him go. And as soon as he knew he was no longer on that hook, he revived and darted away—finally free. And honestly? It was a joy to watch.

I share that story because I see that same desperation in many women's lives—especially women in unsafe and unsustainable marriages. They've "taken the bait" of false hope—and gotten stuck. They're hooked on hope.

Now, let me be clear: *Hope itself isn't bad.* The Bible tells us to hope in the Lord, to wait on Him, and to hold on to His promises. But it also warns us that "Hope deferred makes the heart sick" (Proverbs 13:12).

If you've been clinging to the idea that your marriage *will* change—someday—while year after year nothing improves, then you may be caught in the trap of false hope. Like that catfish, you're not going anywhere, and it's breaking your will to keep going.

Maybe you've been "breadcrumbed" repeatedly. Your husband wounds you, then he apologizes and makes promises to get help… but then the days and months pass, and he goes to one counseling appointment (maybe) and that's it—until the cycle repeats again.

Dear friend, if this all sounds far too familiar, don't settle for less. Real hope is based on real—and repeatable—changes in behavior, proven over an extended period of time. Anything short of this is false hope and can leave you hopeless. God is calling you to release the illusion of change and false promises, and instead anchor yourself in reality. This is where real change can happen. When you do this, you create space for God's truth, His guidance, and His real, lasting freedom to take root in your life.

Prayer:

Dear Father, I've been living on the hook of false hope. I have so longed for my marriage to be healed that I've been willing to believe anything my husband tells me. But I'm not seeing real, lasting change. Please help me to have a radical commitment to

Your truth and my reality. Hold my heart as I take this step and surround me with Your peace and wisdom. Amen.

Reflection:

Where in your life have you been holding onto hope that isn't bringing real change? What broken promises have kept you "hooked" even when nothing improves?

–Pause. Take a deep breath. What's one small step in your healing you– can celebrate today?

Day 28
A Radical Commitment to Reality

"Behold, You desire truth in the inward parts, and in the hidden part You will make me to know wisdom."
Psalm 51:6, NKJV

———*Pause. Take a few deep breaths. Now rest—and abide in Him.*———

By now, you're probably noticing some patterns in your marriage. We've put names on a lot of different destructive behaviors. I understand this may feel hard to accept. And it may feel almost impossible to believe the man who vowed to love you could be the one harming you in these ways, or worse, not willing to stop. But a radical acceptance of what is really happening is the first step toward freedom from these cycles.

Emotional freedom and safety may—or may not—mean separating or leaving the marriage, but it will certainly mean setting better boundaries, speaking your truth in love, and being intentional about keeping yourself and your children emotionally and physically safe. And if you aren't safe, it will mean taking the needed steps to get there.

A radical commitment to reality means we admit the pain that is happening and stop the enabling of sinful behaviors, whether that's no longer minimizing the effects, excusing addictions, or not allowing him to degrade your worth.

If you're in a deceitful, harmful, or abusive marriage, the first step to true healing is honesty about the condition of your marriage. Be brutally honest with yourself. God doesn't want us lying to ourselves; it doesn't honor Him, and it doesn't help us. When we know and accept the truth, His Word promises, "the truth will set you free" (John 8:32).

When we allow our eyes to open to the reality we are living in, it then allows our minds to begin the grieving and healing process.

I know it can be heart-wrenching to realize your dreams of a happy and healthy marriage may not happen, or that you may have a long road to recovery if your marriage is ever going to work. Neither of these is what any woman hopes for when she gets married. I wish I could say there is a better way to start this process... but the truth is the only path to freedom and out of the cycles of chaos, destruction, pain, and deep neglect.

Sweet sister, I know how painful and lonely this can feel. And I know that at times, it can feel easier to ignore it and hope the pain will just go away. I even understand that setting boundaries and naming your husband's behavior as unsafe can feel unloving.

But the truth is, naming our reality, even the painful parts, is an act of love. This is the most loving thing you can do for yourself, your children, and even for your husband. God doesn't want your husband drowning in his sin, any more than He wants you and your children to be hurt by it. God tells us He desires us to live in truth in our inward parts (Psalm 51:6).

It's natural to grieve the loss of what you hoped your marriage could be. It's OK to feel the heaviness of your current truth. God sees your every tear and longs to walk with you and guide you as you find your way to freedom. Because His Word promises He will never leave you nor forsake you—even if others have (Deuteronomy 31:6).

Prayer:

Dear Father, I bring You my tears and my pain. I bring You the reality of my marriage as it is, not as I hope it will be someday. Help me to see the truth of my marriage in its fullness. And hold my heart as You do. I give You my shattered dreams and my hurting heart. Please give me the courage and strength to live in truth and not in denial. And help me to walk toward Your freedom. Amen.

Reflection:

What is the honest reality of your marriage? How long have these patterns existed and how have they affected you and your children? Where have you been minimizing or excusing harmful behavior, and what truth do you need to acknowledge today? What does having a radical commitment to reality mean for you?

–Pause. Take a deep breath. What's one small step in your healing you can celebrate today?

Day 29

Exposing Shame to the Light

"But everything exposed by the light becomes visible—and everything that is illuminated becomes a light."

Ephesians 5:13

———*Pause. Take a few deep breaths. Now rest—and abide in Him.*———

You may have grown up in a home that was chaotic, unsafe, or filled with wounds that no one tended to. Maybe shame seeped into your being before you even knew what to call it. Or, you grew up in a family that everyone called "healthy," "respectable," or "well-off," and yet you still carry a private ache you can't name.

You can come from a long line of "brokenness," or you can come from a line that looks polished and put-together and shame still finds ways to enter. Shame travels through generations.

You could have been raised in a Christian home and still feel shame's grip smothering you. You may now be married to the pastor, teach Bible studies, host the gatherings, raise children who always seem to say the right things—and yet, when you crawl in bed at night you feel shame curling up beside you.

On the outside, we can look steady, but inside, shame can be dismantling our God-given identity piece by piece.

Some of us were taught from childhood to see ourselves as the problem—too loud, too needy, too emotional, too sensitive, too much—or worse, not enough. Never enough.

Shame is subtle; that's its power. It doesn't announce itself; it burrows. It hides in the corners of our minds, in the stories we won't touch, or in the habits we cling to because they once helped us to survive.

Shame wraps itself around us like an old security blanket—familiar, trusted, protective at first. But woven into that blanket are barbs we can't see. And the more we pull it close, the more it cuts.

Shame enters families quietly. A story never told. A wound never acknowledged. A trauma packed so tightly and deep that it seeps out years later as something completely unrecognizable. An unhealthy coping mechanism that becomes a family's new "normal." A culture of silence that slowly becomes a legacy.

Sadly, many families live under an unspoken rule: "We don't talk about that." We don't name what happened. We don't disrupt the family "image." We pretend. We protect secrets. We think we're suppressing something.

But instead, that shame travels—from one generation to the next, from one wounded soul to another. Shaping us in ways we can't see, until the damage is already done.

Mary DeMuth says it well: "An untold story never heals." Because our untold stories don't just sit quietly tucked away in the dark recesses of our being, they grow. They grow into beliefs about who we are, what we deserve, and how small we must stay.

A painful past will do one of two things: It will either make us wiser, stronger, more grounded and gracious. Or it will teach us to hide, to shrink, to numb, or abandon ourselves so others can feel comfortable.

A painful wound or past can become the pedestal that lifts us to higher ground, *not because* the pain was good, but because God transformed it. Or it can become the pedestal we trip over again and again, the same one that sends us sprawling into deeper shame, convincing us we're incapable of walking forward.

Guilt says, I did something wrong. From there, we can work on doing better. But shame says: Something is wrong with me.

Left unchecked, shame can erode our sense of worth, even our identity. It seeps into every corner, whispering at first—*You're not good enough. Don't try. Remember how you failed?*

But it never stays a whisper. Soon it shouts. It locks doors of opportunity. It corrodes relationships. It convinces you to settle for less than the good God has waiting for you. It tells you that the story you fear is the story you must never speak.

But here's the radical truth that the adversary doesn't want you to discover: Your story is not the enemy. Silence is.

"But everything exposed by the light becomes visible—and everything that is illuminated becomes a light" (Ephesians 5:13).

Dear friend, God's Word promises that when we allow the painful pieces of our past or present to be brought into His light, He doesn't shame us—He transforms us. He takes what was once hidden and uses it to illuminate the darkness. He uses what was once a wound to bring healing to you and often to others as well.

While shame can travel through generations when it's left unchecked, so can healing when it's brought into the light.

Prayer:

Dear Father, help me bring all things into the light. Meet me there to heal any hidden wounds so that I can move forward stronger and healthier in You. Amen.

Reflection:

What things have left the sting of shame in your soul? Have you brought these things to the light by sharing them with a safe person? If not, who could you do that with now?

–Pause. Take a deep breath. What's one small step in your healing you can celebrate today?

Day 30
Being Present in the Unkempt Spaces

"Arise and eat, because the journey is too great for you."
1 Kings 19:7

——*Pause. Take a few deep breaths. Now rest—and abide in Him.*——

One morning, three days before my court date to obtain a restraining order, I felt numb—torn between the vows I had spoken years earlier and the reality I could no longer deny.

I woke feeling exhausted from the aching in my heart, the stress that lived in my body, and the hyper-vigilance of feeling like I had to protect my safety and sanity.

I dragged myself out of bed and stumbled into the bathroom, ready to try to "pick myself up" with a shower. I was doing my best to take that "one next right step."

But instead, I paused. I stood there in the bathroom and took stock. I allowed myself to really see what was in front of me—to be present, which is something survival mode *rarely* affords.

I took stock of the drain that had not been dealt with for months. I took stock of the "snake" device that had been left there for me to clear the clogged drain. I took stock of the fact that I had been bathing each and every day in a dirty tub, because the drain backed up *every time* I took a shower—and I never took the time to clear it.

In that moment, I realized I had been letting my circumstances overwhelm me to the point that I wasn't taking responsibility for what was mine to handle. A bit of a victim mentality had taken over. And while I truly had been a victim and was feeling the weight and unfairness of having to go to court just to have peace, God was whispering a different truth to me: "It's time to move from victim to survivor." But to do that, I had to use the agency He had given me to take the steps necessary for what was right in front of me.

For the last few months, that shower had become my last stand. I simply was not tackling one more problem—even if it meant showering in ankle-deep water! Sometimes we just need to have grace on ourselves. Those few months were such a time for me.

But then, there are also times when that little unkempt corner of our life needs to be addressed as a part of our healing. And that morning, God spoke to me in that still, small voice and said: "The rest of your day can wait. Be present here in this unkempt space for a moment."

So, there I stood, undressed and debating my next move. Finally, I surrendered my plans. I knew my idea of being refreshed with a shower held no real reassurance of working, anyway!

There I was, in my birthday suit with snake in hand, *being present*. On my hands and knees, I painstakingly worked the hair out of that drain. I know this isn't a pretty image, but stay with me! Strand by strand, I stayed present. I showed up. I did what I felt my Father calling me to do: "The one next right thing."

In that small window of time, I stopped thinking about my pain and even my fear of going to court. Instead, I focused on showing up and engaging my agency to do something productive that could make me feel better in the long run.

That messy tub had become an indicator of the overwhelm of my heart. It had become the outward sign of my inward paralysis.

With each new clump of bedraggled, filthy muck I pulled from the drain, the strangest thing happened: I felt a sense of hope. First, just hope that I would no longer be standing in ankle deep water every time I took a shower! But then, another small glimmer of hope—that I *would* be able to put back the pieces of my life. One small step at a time. And it started with addressing that one unkempt space.

In that moment, God was showing me, as He had shown Elijah, when He told him "rise and eat" in the midst of his despair and fear, that sometimes even the smallest gesture of moving forward is all we need to get back on track and to start being present in our life again. Take the one next right step today, dear friend. We've got this.

Prayer:

Dear Lord, please show me where I need to be present in my life. Guide me as I go through this journey to stay grounded in the here and the now, and help me not to be thrust into the future with worry or into the past with regret. Thank You for walking with me. Amen.

Reflection:

What are some unkempt spaces you feel God calling you to take care of? Where is God inviting you to be more present in your life? Is it in your home, with your kiddos, in your quiet time, or with your friends? What small act of presence could bring you a little more peace today?

—Pause. Take a deep breath. What's one small step in your healing you can celebrate today?

Day 31

Boundaries Are Biblical

"But one thing is needed, and Mary has chosen that good part, which will not be taken away from her."
Luke 10:42, NKJV

―――*Pause. Take a few deep breaths. Now rest—and abide in Him.*―――

I want to share the story of Martha with you. Martha grew up in a home where her parents' relationship was non-functioning. Her father drank, and her mother worked two jobs to keep life afloat, often turning Martha into her counselor for her marriage problems. From a young age, Martha was "parentified"—caring for siblings, managing her mom and dad's emotions, and keeping the household together.

As she grew up, Martha never learned where she ended and others began, which left her with weak boundaries. She was always serving and often sacrificing her needs so she could please others. Years later, she found herself in a marriage that mirrored the chaos of her childhood.

Her husband manipulated, gaslit, and controlled her, all while cloaking it in religion. Adding insult to injury, he spent his nights consuming pornography, which he hid for years.

Her marriage began to feel like a prison. Yet, Martha's instinct was to sacrifice her peace to keep the home stable, just as she had done as a child. Boundaries were foreign to her. They felt mean and selfish, because on some level she felt pity for everyone else's dysfunction.

Martha often cited Scriptures, like "Honor your father and mother" or "Submit to your husband" as reasons to acquiesce to others. She unknowingly used faith to give up her own well-being. Martha had become a martyr for other people's sins. And this was often cemented in the messages she heard at church. So, she tried harder, gave more, prayed more, and continued to expect little. This left her bitter inside.

But here's the truth that Martha slowly learned: We are not responsible for other people's sins or dysfunction. We can't control them or save them. We can pray for them and love them, but salvation and change are ultimately God's work—*and* the other person's choice.

Dear friend, if you find yourself in any part of Martha's story, please hear this: Boundaries are not mean; they are biblical and life-giving. They protect our hearts from cruelty, manipulation, and control. They help us to take responsibility for our own "stuff," while we allow others to own theirs. And they protect our ability to love well without getting worn out.

Without healthy boundaries, we risk overextending ourselves continually until we're burned out and responding in anger, rather than being proactive and responding calmly but firmly. It is possible to give kind boundaries that don't change who we are or cause us to come down to the same level of dysfunction.

Just as Martha learned to stop over-functioning, we're told of another Martha, in the Bible, who learned the same lesson. We can be so busy with other people's messes that we don't even have time for what Scripture calls the "good part": sitting at the feet of Jesus. We, too, may need to step back from over-functioning while those around us under-function—and, in doing so, create space to abide in the One who can bring our hearts peace (Luke 10:38-42).

Practical boundaries might look like saying no to demands that drain you, limiting contact with those who wound you, or giving consequences if someone's harmful behaviors don't stop: like addictions, anger, pornography use, or control. When we do this, we reclaim our peace, protect our joy, and restore our ability to love others well, without losing ourselves.

God wants good for you, sweet friend. Don't let the dysfunction of others steal that from you. Don't allow anyone to distract you from the peace, purpose, and wholeness you deserve. Sit with the One who is calling you to that "good part."

Prayer:

Dear Heavenly Father, I've been wearing myself thin by over-functioning while others around me under-function. Please help me, like Mary, tend to my own soul's needs first, so I can truly show up as my best self. Amen.

Reflection:

Where in life do you need to stop over-functioning for others—in your marriage, in your friendships, in your work, at church? Where do you need to practice saying no or setting better boundaries? What's one realistic boundary you could set that honors your peace and healing?

–Pause. Take a deep breath. What's one small step in your healing you can celebrate today?

Day 32
The Power of Saying No

"All you need to say is simply 'Yes' or 'No.'"
Matthew 5:37

——*Pause. Take a few deep breaths. Now rest—and abide in Him.*——

For years, I believed my husband's angry outbursts were beyond his control. He often told me he didn't mean to hurt us, and I wanted to believe him. But over time, I realized a painful truth. Sometimes when he yelled, I either called someone for help or drew attention to the situation—and he would instantly calm himself. His anger wasn't uncontrollable—it was a choice, which he could turn off for others, but not for us.

Through my own counseling and learning more about abuse, I understood his problem wasn't anger—it was control. He insisted he never intentionally hurt us, but his actions told a different story: He *could* regulate his emotions depending on the audience.

The hardest part was that our marriage, like many unsafe or unsustainable marriages, had "good times," too. But even those were often overshadowed by smaller incidents that left lasting scars. Trips that should have been joyful were marred by raging or lingering anger, silent treatments, tension, jumping out of cars on the side of a highway, or last-minute angry cancellations. These mixed experiences and constant unpredictably made it confusing to name the truth—and left us walking on eggshells.

In working with women, I often hear this same pattern: Their husbands only "lose control" or behave rudely or in controlling ways with them—never with others.

Scripture warns about this kind of emotional volatility:

"Do not make friends with a hot-tempered person, do not associate with one easily angered, or you may learn their ways and get yourself ensnared" (Proverbs 22:24-25).

Setting boundaries in this kind of environment can feel confusing. You know it's not likely your husband will accept them, especially if he's benefited from your previous lack of limits.

"Boundary pushers" (and breakers) come in many types—guilt trippers, manipulators, and even dangerous individuals who react with anger and violence when they feel like they're losing control. People with narcissistic personality traits often fall into this last category.

This can keep you stuck for fear of how your spouse will respond. But it's important to remember you can't control how anyone responds to your boundaries.

They *may* reject, punish, or blame you—so your fears may not be unfounded. But if it's an important boundary to you, standing firm is essential—*if it is safe to do so*. Boundaries only work when you follow through; without consequences, they become suggestions.

You are not the bad guy for expressing your truth or your needs. Even if he blames, shames, or uses DARVO to silence you, you deserve respect. You are not unloving for protecting your heart or your children.

God calls us to live in truth, even when it's uncomfortable—but in a safe way. Boundaries help protect you and your children and teach others how to treat you. Trust God to guide you, seek help when you need clarity on boundaries, and allow Him to walk with you as you reclaim your voice, your peace, and your freedom.

Prayer:

Dear Heavenly Father, teach me how to set wise boundaries, lead me to resources that walk me through the specifics, and give me the peace to know You are with me. Amen.

Reflection:

When your boundaries are broken, how do you normally respond? What consequences do you give and do you follow through on them?

Depending on your situation, you may find the "grey rock" method helpful. It's a strategy that involves calmly responding to manipulative, narcissistic, or boundary-pushing behaviors with minimal emotion or engagement. This approach can help you protect your peace and avoid being drawn into unnecessary conflict.

I've also included other resources on boundaries and navigating arguments in the back of the book for further reading.

Note: If your situation has involved violence or threats of danger, prayerfully prepare a Safety Plan (link in the back of the book) before expressing your boundaries. Learn how to protect yourself and your children before speaking your truth. In some cases, you may need to immediately and quietly move to safety without confrontation first. Ask God for wisdom and discernment in each step you take and seek someone to help walk you through the safest way to start setting boundaries.

–Pause. Take a deep breath. What's one small step in your healing you can celebrate today?

Day 33
The Lies that Keep Us Stuck

"Then you will know the truth, and the truth will set you free."
John 8:32

———*Pause. Take a few deep breaths. Now rest—and abide in Him.*———

Dear friend, there may be some untruths that are keeping you trapped in dysfunction. The enemy loves to whisper lies to us, but his deceptions are often predictable. He likes to isolate us so we can't compare notes with others. So, let's pull up a chair and talk honestly.

I'll share a lie (or partial lie) that many of us have believed, and then a truth I hope you can begin to internalize.[1] Remember that when we allow ourselves to see the truth, the truth can set us free (John 8:32).

Lie: God wants me to forgive and forget. **Truth**: Scripture calls us to forgive, not forget. God gave us minds to remember danger for a reason: to protect ourselves. If harmful behaviors are still happening, you're not keeping "a record of wrongs," you're being wise to take note. That's not the past you're recording, it's the present.

Lie: He's had a hard life; he can't help that he struggles. **Truth:** Many people have endured hardships, but not all choose to cheat, abuse, or destroy families.

Lie: I need to wait, things will get better when "xyz" happens. **Truth:** It's likely you've seen enough. Waiting for more evidence, a change in your circumstances, or a miracle isn't the priority—your healing and safety are.

Lie: But he loves me and doesn't mean to hurt me. **Truth:** Love doesn't cause repeated harm. He may say he loves you, but if he did, he'd do everything in his power to protect you, not hurt you.

Lie: We both have issues. **Truth:** While self-awareness is good, abuse, addiction, and betrayal are not two-way streets. Your struggles are not equivalent to being repeatedly betrayed or abused.

Lie: He's really trying. **Truth:** Maybe he is, but if you're still being hurt repeatedly, then there's still a problem. So, you need to ask, "How long am I willing to keep getting wounded?"

Lie: I'm just over-reacting. **Truth:** Take a step back for a moment. If a friend were in your shoes, would you tell her that? Consider the impact on your health, your children, and your life.

Lie: If I work harder, things will get better. **Truth:** I imagine you've *already* tried changing—patience, prayer, submission, and maybe even changing who you are to keep the peace. Your change will not guarantee his.

Lie: Other people have it worse than me, he's never hit me. **Truth:** While others may have experienced a different form of hurt in their marriage that doesn't negate the pain and confusion in yours.

Lie: He's a good person at heart. **Truth:** He may be, but good intentions don't erase the impact of his hurtful actions.

There are other lies, too: "I'm too weak to leave." "It's all my fault." "No one will believe me." "Divorce will destroy my kids." Or "I'll never be loved again."

While some of these may feel true in the moment, many women have found safety, support, and even joy after speaking their truth, learning to set boundaries, or separating from an unsafe or unsustainable marriage. Planning and seeking help make it possible to protect yourself and your children.

Sweet friend, I know this feels heavy. But you're not alone. God sees your pain and wants to help guide you to safety, wisdom, and restoration. Start by naming the lies, affirming the truth, and taking one small step toward your healing. Each step matters.

Prayer:

Dear Father, please help me to determine what lies I may be telling myself. Help me to walk in the truth and to find freedom in that truth. Thank You for guiding me and opening my eyes so I can begin to gain strength emotionally, physically, and spiritually.

Reflection:

What lies have you been telling yourself—about your marriage, your husband, yourself, or your situation? What truth can you replace them with?

—Pause. Take a deep breath. What's one small step in your healing you can celebrate today?

Day 34
Sacred Body: Sexual Boundaries

"Do you not know that your bodies are temples of the Holy Spirit, who is in you, whom you have received from God?"

1 Corinthians 6:19

———*Pause. Take a few deep breaths. Now rest—and abide in Him.*———

Scripture tells us our bodies are temples—sacred places (1 Corinthians 6:19). And as such, we should expect others to treat them that way.

God designed marital intimacy to flow from connection, trust, and emotional safety—not fear, manipulation, or betrayal. God designed sex to be rooted in emotional connection. Without that foundation, sexual intimacy can feel disconnected, leaving you feeling like just a tool for someone else's pleasure—and that's not the "being known" God speaks of in the Bible.

In marriage, God said the two would become one flesh, not that one person should satisfy their flesh at the expense of the other's feelings and emotions. Yes, God also created sex for pleasure—but for *both* partners. How can your body ever relax if you're constantly on emotional guard, whether inside or outside the bedroom?

If your husband is soliciting sex outside of marriage, having an affair, or harming you sexually, protect yourself; it is biblically appropriate to set a protective boundary around sexual intimacy.

It's also healthy to set a boundary around the bedroom if you're being abused in other ways or your husband is harming your children. If you find yourself tearful after being intimate because your heart is being repeatedly wounded, this is not true intimacy.

However, be prepared. Despite what some may say, setting a boundary is not an instant solution—and in this case, it almost certainly won't be. With people who don't respect your boundaries, peace rarely comes right away. Often, boundaries bring resistance and may even spark disagreements.

If your husband has always been allowed to treat you however he pleases—emotionally or physically—while continuing to have access to your body, this new boundary most likely will *not* go over well.

He may respond with guilt-trips, gaslighting, or anger. He may even try to use the Bible to tell you that God doesn't approve of you withholding sex, until he can treat you with respect. But that doesn't make your boundary wrong—God is far more concerned about the things your husband is doing to harm you, than his need for sex.

Boundaries mark the beginning of a courageous yet uncomfortable journey. They shake foundations, expose long-standing imbalances, and invite resistance. Boundaries can upset people, but they are often the clearest way to show someone their actions are hurting us.

But please hear this, sweet friend: His reaction is not your responsibility. Your peace, your safety, your healing, and your wholeness are. When someone has shown they can't be trusted with your heart, it's both wise and necessary to adjust the access they have to it. And if, over time, they begin to demonstrate genuine change and trustworthiness, that access can be adjusted accordingly.

Even Jesus set boundaries. He walked away from the crowds. He rested. He didn't entrust Himself to everyone (John 2:24). He loved wisely. And He calls us to do the same.

This is not about being vindictive or mean. It may sound like it, but boundaries done right are never about harming someone else—they're about protecting our dignity and our peace.

You are doing the hard, holy work of safeguarding your soul and body—and God honors that.

Each step you take in regaining your voice is important. God meets you even in the messy parts of this journey and invites you to keep reaching for His hand. He is there to hold you steady.

Prayer:

Dear Father, this journey has not been easy. I've been hurt and wounded by my husband, and I don't know how to be intimate when my soul feels broken. Help me to grieve the loss of healthy sexual intimacy in my marriage. Please guide me as I try to protect myself and grow into the woman of God You are shaping me to be. Amen.

Reflection:

Reflect on your current emotional, physical, and spiritual safety in your marriage. Does sexual intimacy in your marriage feel healthy and mutual? Is your husband withdrawing intimacy as punishment or expecting sex while he continues to hurt you emotionally? What are some small steps you can take to protect your body, mind, and soul?

—Pause. Take a deep breath. What's one small step in your healing you—can celebrate today?

Day 35
Safe Stewardship: Establishing Financial Safety

"But whoever gathers money little by little makes it grow."
Proverbs 13:11

———*Pause. Take a few deep breaths. Now rest—and abide in Him.*———

Lisa never seemed to have enough money to go around. Her kiddos were wearing clothes they outgrew two seasons ago, and she shopped at thrift stores for her own clothes. She drove an old vehicle, while her husband drove a new one. Yet, her husband gave generously to missions and church projects.

He recently shared an idea "God laid on his heart." He would give away half of his paycheck each week so they could "test" God's faithfulness. He passionately explained to Lisa that "God honors the faithful." Meanwhile, she was budgeting every penny of her small allowance and still coming up short. Lisa felt stretched, anxious, and unsure of how she could safeguard herself and her children financially.

Your situation may be different, but the power imbalance and unfairness still feel familiar. Maybe your husband makes major purchases without consulting you. Or maybe you carry the financial burden—working, caring for the kids, holding everything together while he squanders money on his addiction. Or maybe there's no obvious financial abuse, but deep down, you know you need to create a safety net—just in case you ever need to leave.

This is a tender space between where you are and where you know you need to be. I know it can feel uncomfortable when you don't know exactly what financial safety looks like or how to get there. But what if this is just a "turning point"—one more place where you begin to pivot toward something healthier?

Please hear me when I say this: Saving for an unknown future is not disloyalty to your husband, and it's not selfish—it's wise. Being a biblical help meet does not mean God created you to enable your husband's poor or selfish choices. That's not your calling. God calls you to walk in wisdom and truth.

Creating financial stability isn't you being sneaky or rebellious; it's about protecting yourself and your children—and walking in discernment. Financial insecurity can feel paralyzing—and God doesn't want you living in fear.

In fact, Scripture teaches us to be wise stewards. Proverbs 13:11 says: "But whoever gathers money little by little makes it grow." And Proverbs 21:20: "The wise store up choice food and olive oil." And one of my favorite verses about money, Proverbs 6:6-8 says: "Go to the ant... consider its ways and be wise! It has no commander, no overseer or ruler, yet it stores its provisions in summer and gathers its food at harvest."

You don't need an overseer or permission to be wise with what God gives you. But maybe right now, you don't have much to work with. That's OK. The ant starts each season with nothing; we all start somewhere.

Maybe this is a time of small beginnings—finding a job for side income, opening a private account "to store your provisions," or connecting with an outreach that helps women build financial security. Pray and ask God to guide you.

As you take that one next step, confidence begins to grow. Be like that little ant—faithful, diligent, and wise. Your prudence is not deception; it's faith in action. It's saying to yourself, "I am going to take the steps to get healthy and safe." And in doing so, you honor what God entrusts you with and prepare for a more stable, secure future—just like that little ant.

Prayer:

Dear Father, I've been struggling to know what my next steps should be. Please give me wisdom to see how I can become more financially secure and prepare for whatever may happen if my marriage continues to struggle. Help me trust Your leading each step of the way. Amen.

Reflection:

Reflect on one or two practical steps you can take to begin building financial stability and security for your future.

–Pause. Take a deep breath. What's one small step in your healing you can celebrate today?

Day 36
Grieving What is Lost

"Blessed are those who mourn, for they will be comforted."
Matthew 5:4

———*Pause. Take a few deep breaths. Now rest—and abide in Him.*———

Any time we experience a deep loss or a death, grief follows. We readily acknowledge the need to grieve the death of a beloved friend or family member. But we don't always acknowledge the need to grieve other endings.

By now you may feel an ache in your heart over the marriage you hoped you would have. The reality that your marriage isn't healthy—or maybe even safe—can be painful to face. It's a loss. The loss of a dream. The dream of having a loving partner, a peaceful home, someone to grow old with who will cherish you.

You may even be grieving the fact that your husband may not change. Your grief may come while you're still in your marriage, or it may surface once you've left. You may need to grieve both the person you thought your spouse was and the pain they caused.

It's important to give yourself permission to walk through the grieving process—all of it.

Be gentle with yourself. It can be tempting to minimize your losses or compare them to what others have gone through. Sometimes we even try to rush past the pain with thoughts like, *God has a plan, so I just need to move on.* Or, *My pain surely isn't as bad as what others have gone through.* But, dear friend, your pain is real, your loss is deep, and your grief is valid.

Try not to shame yourself for what naturally surfaces. God doesn't. "He is near to the brokenhearted and saves those who are crushed in spirit" (Psalm 34:18). If you ever doubt that God is with you in your grief, open the Psalms—it's filled with pages of raw lament. God honors our tears and listens with the intent to heal.

You may even feel disoriented about the future, and wonder, "Who am I now, if not a wife?" It might feel like your very identity has been lost. That ache you feel is part of the past unraveling, so something new can grow.

Grief isn't tidy. It's not just one emotion, it's more like a winding path through many. Each emotion that comes has a purpose and can teach you something about what you've endured. Shock, anger over the injustice, sorrow for what was lost, fear of what's ahead, even relief for what's behind you now. Each one has its place. Let them come, in their time, and once they've done their work, gently let them pass.

Don't be afraid of this part of your story; it's here for your healing. God made your tears for a purpose—they cleanse the soul and soften our hearts to make room for new life.

When you allow yourself to feel what's true instead of suppressing it, you make space for wholeness to return, slowly, gently, and in its time. Authenticity leads to stability. And God meets us right where we are when we get real with Him.

"Weeping may endure for a night, but joy *comes* in the morning" (Psalm 30:5, NKJV, emphasis added). God doesn't rush the night, but He will stay with you in it, no matter how dark, until the first light of morning begins to rise.

Prayer:

God, please help me learn from each emotion, and when its work is done, help me to release it. Keep me from getting stuck in places You've already called me to move beyond but also give me the courage to enter into what I've been afraid to feel. Please meet me in my grief and lead me toward Your peace. Amen.

Reflection:

What do you need to grieve today? Is it the loss of your marriage, or maybe the way you hoped your marriage could be? Are you grieving the loss of friendships that were part of your connected social circle, or maybe even your home or your pets if you've had to leave?

–Pause. Take a deep breath. What's one small step in your healing you– can celebrate today?

Day 37

How to Know When Change is Real

"For the kind of sorrow God wants us to experience leads us away from sin and results in salvation."
2 Corinthians 7:10, NLT

——Pause. Take a few deep breaths. Now rest—and abide in Him.——

As I've been writing this devotional, I've been thinking of you—and my heart aches for what you might be walking through. I know firsthand that one of the hardest parts of this journey is admitting what's really happening. We want to believe every glimmer of change means the nightmare is finally over—that our life can go back to normal. Deep down, we fear the truth. If nothing is really changing, our world might have to. And that's terrifying.

It takes enormous courage to face that reality. You are doing a brave thing.

So, take a deep breath, friend. You're not alone in this. Let's walk through together what real change looks like.

The word we're really talking about here is *repentance*. In the Greek text used in the Bible, this means "a change of mind and direction"—a turning away from the sin and back toward God.

The Apostle Paul was dealing with some very difficult behaviors going on in the church in Corinth. They were divisive, prideful, and sexually immoral—like the man who was sexually involved with his father's wife (1 Corinthians 5:1). Anger, hypocrisy, pride, narcissism, sexual issues, porn, hidden affairs—maybe some of this feels familiar in your marriage.

Paul didn't want to confront them (2 Corinthians 2:4), but he knew he had to. Maybe you feel that way, too—you don't want to confront your husband, but you know you need to.

When Paul wrote his difficult letter, the Corinthians didn't just respond back with a quick "I'm sorry"—they truly repented. And in 2 Corinthians 7:10-11 (NLT), Paul describes what their true repentance looked like versus what worldly sorrow looks like.

> For the kind of sorrow God wants us to experience leads us away from sin and results in salvation… But worldly sorrow, which lacks repentance, results in spiritual death. Just see what this godly sorrow produced in you! Such earnestness, such concern to clear yourselves, such indignation, such alarm, such longing to see me, such zeal, and such a readiness to punish wrong. You showed that you have done everything necessary to make things right.

Worldly sorrow says, "I'm sorry I got caught." It's tears and promises, but no lasting change.

Godly sorrow, though, grieves the damage caused and allows God to transform the heart. This leads to lasting change.

True repentance looks like:

- He takes ownership, understanding his behaviors without excuses or blame.
- He's alarmed by who he *was* and committed to lasting change.
- He shows deep empathy and grief for your pain—not briefly, but consistently.
- He gives you space and time to heal, without pressuring you to "move on."

So ask yourself: Is he more upset about appearances, his reputation, or the fallout of being caught? Or is he broken over the pain he's caused you *and* how it's affecting his own heart and walk with God? Does he want quick relief for himself—or complete healing and restoration for you and himself?

Real change isn't just words—it's about a heart turned toward God and actions that prove it over time. I know this isn't easy, sweet friend, but remember—living in truth is always better than avoiding what's real. Truth is where freedom begins. God sees your courage and the strength it takes to face what's real and not settle for half-hearted change. Lean into Him as you walk toward healing and wholeness.

Prayer:

Dear Father, my heart is heavy. It's been a long road and I'm tired of trying to make sense of it all. Hold me close as I keep taking brave steps toward healing—whether my husband chooses to or not. Help me trust that You will guide me into Your truth, peace, and freedom. Amen.

Reflection:

Take a quiet moment and look at the more detailed list of what true repentance looks like (see the link in the Resources section at the back of the devotional). Ask yourself honestly: Am I seeing the fruit of real, godly change—or just signs of worldly sorrow?

–Pause. Take a deep breath. What's one small step in your healing you can celebrate today?

Day 38

When Keeping the Peace Becomes an Idol

"Am I now seeking the approval of man, or of God?"
Galatians 1:10, ESV

———*Pause. Take a few deep breaths. Now rest—and abide in Him.*———

Years ago, a counselor asked me a question, one that completely floored me. Honestly, I initially found it confusing. She said, "Is it possible that you've made your husband an idol?"

I had to really think about her question and finally concluded that, yes, I had. Keeping the peace, guarding my heart, and trying to figure out what was happening controlled my every waking moment. I had placed my marriage and my husband ahead of everything else in my life, even before my relationship with God.

Maybe you find yourself in this place, too. Anything that takes the place of God in our hearts can become our idol. Sometimes it's not just our spouse we make an idol—it's peace itself. We sacrifice our truth, our identity, and even our walk with God just to avoid conflict. We cling to what feels safe, instead of to God, who holds us secure.

I did anything I could to please and agree with my husband, because it meant peace—at least for the moment. I was desperate to please him, because I feared if I didn't, he wouldn't give me affection, he wouldn't treat me well, or it could trigger another disagreement.

Maybe for you it looks like being afraid to speak up, being afraid to set boundaries for fear of his response, or even holding back your opinion because it doesn't align with his.

But pleasing someone else to the detriment of our own beliefs, values, and even opinions stops us from showing up as our authentic selves. It turns us into people-pleasers who fear rejection more than we follow God. And we lose ourselves in the mix and miss out on the joy of living as God's beloved daughters, full of our own unique thoughts and opinions. When you notice yourself doing this, let it be an invitation to discern what's really happening. Taking note is the first step to responding differently.

God is calling you out of fear and into His freedom. He doesn't want us paralyzed but anchored in His love—that's where we can know our worth and walk in truth. God is asking each of us today: "Am I now seeking the approval of man, or of God?" (Galatians 1:10, ESV). And if our answer is man, He is calling to our hearts: "Fear not, for I have redeemed you, I have called you by my name, you are mine" (Isaiah 43:1, ESV).

Dear friend, if you've been silencing yourself to avoid conflict, you weren't meant to live that way—unless, of course, that silence is protecting you until you get to a safe place. God's perfect love drives out fear (1 John 4:18). Pray for Him to give you the courage to live as His beloved daughter in the fullness of all that means, and not as someone else's shadow.

Prayer:

Dear Father, help me not to give in to people pleasing, but to stand firm in Your love and who You made me to be. Help me to learn who I am, what I believe, and the values You have written on my heart. Teach me to find my worth, security, and rest in You alone. Amen.

Reflection:

Where have you been giving up parts of yourself in order to keep the peace or earn your husband's approval or affection? What small steps can you take to begin honoring who God created you to be, instead of shrinking to avoid conflict?

–Pause. Take a deep breath. What's one small step in your healing you–can celebrate today?

Day 39

The Impact of Abuse and Betrayal on Decision Making

"I will instruct you and teach you in the way you should go; I will counsel you with my loving eye on you."
Psalm 32:8

——*Pause. Take a few deep breaths. Now rest—and abide in Him.*——

Trauma and abuse can take a toll on our ability to make decisions. When we're repeatedly forced into fight, flight, freeze, or fawn mode, our amygdala, aka our brain's alarm system, stays on high alert. It's trying to warn us of danger, and sometimes it's right. But this constant activation throws our prefrontal cortex—the part of our brain responsible for reasoning, problem-solving, and planning—offline. Suddenly, thinking clearly feels impossible.

Add in gaslighting, blame-shifting, or endless arguments meant to confuse, and we start doubting ourselves. We may also freeze under pressure or feel "foggy" when trying to process even the simplest information. Over time, this can lead to learned helplessness—the sense that no matter what you do, nothing changes, so why try?

For many women, this confusion is compounded by spiritual pressure. Family or church messages like "just be patient," "just submit more," or "just pray harder" can keep you circling around the same pain without ever addressing the root cause—the destructive behavior.

When verses like "God hates divorce" or "Wives, submit to your husbands" are taken out of context, they can create shame or paralyze you with fear of making the wrong decision. You may even start to believe that protecting yourself and your children is somehow sinning against God.

But, friend, that is not the heart of God. When your mind and soul are under siege, He does not shame you for seeking clarity or safety. He knows that space from the chaos—space to breathe—is *exactly* what allows your nervous system to rest so clarity can come. And when your nervous system is able to rest and not be on high alert this allows your body and mind to begin to heal.

Safety restores reasoning. Healing renews wisdom. And this is where the fog starts to lift.

When I reached the point in my marriage where I could no longer think clearly because my nervous system was stuck on high alert, I realized I had two choices: continue as things had always been or trust God as I stepped away to gain clarity.

It started small at first—with walks alone to clear my head. Then came time apart for a day or two to journal and reflect. As clarity grew, I began to see what I had really been living in. I was creating space to grieve, to think clearly, and to heal.

As I did this, I noticed how different my body and mind felt during these reprieves from dysfunction and tension. Eventually, I grew healthy enough to think through solid boundaries and confident enough to set consequences when those boundaries were trespassed.

The time apart helped me see that my husband wasn't changing—but I had been. I had become hopeless, depressed, and was on the brink of giving up. Creating space allowed me to think my own thoughts without being told what to think.

In time, as I gained strength and perspective, I knew I had to step away more permanently. Time and space had made it clear that lasting change wasn't going to happen.

Separation provided the emotional safety and physical healing I needed to think clearly again. God wants this for us. He gave us these minds, and He doesn't want us to let anyone degrade them.

I hope this for you, too, because you deserve to feel peace and clarity. God longs for you to experience His calm, to think clearly, and to live from a place of truth instead of confusion. Dear friend, I encourage you to create the space you need to process and heal so that God can renew your strength and guide your steps.

Prayer:

Dear God, I have felt so confused and paralyzed. Some days I wonder if I should leave, and other days I cling to hope for a miracle. Please help me to create the space I need to think clearly, away from the chaos and pain. Give me wisdom, peace, and courage to make decisions and to trust that I am capable of doing so. Amen.

Reflection:

What has been confusing for you? Are you waiting to see if change will come or bracing for more hurt—another betrayal, more porn, or controlling behaviors? What's one small step you can take to create space so your nervous system can settle and you can think more clearly? (Reminder: When your mind feels foggy or anxious, deep breathing can calm your body and help you make grounded decisions.)

—Pause. Take a deep breath. What's one small step in your healing you can celebrate today?

Day 40
Your Body is Not Broken

*"A cheerful heart is good medicine,
but a crushed spirit dries up the bones."*
Proverbs 17:22

——*Pause. Take a few deep breaths. Now rest—and abide in Him.*——

There was a time when I was in and out of doctors' offices so much, I felt like my body had become a road map of pins and needles as the doctors searched for what was wrong with me. But nobody ever asked me how my heart and soul were doing—those were left out in the lobby.

I was constantly tired, losing clumps of hair, and dealing with stomach, bladder, heart, and allergy issues—the list seemed endless. What neither I nor the doctors realized was that my body was keeping the score of what was happening in our home.

I've heard this from countless other women, too. Many have even shared that their mystery ailments improved—or went away—once they stepped away from the stress and chaos in their marriages.

Our bodies are fearfully and wonderfully made, but they're meant to be treated with gentleness and care. And when they aren't, they break down.

Trauma gets stored in our bodies. Abuse, constant stress, and betrayal can lock our nervous system in survival mode. Hyper-vigilance exhausts the body, and over time stress can lead to chronic pain, illness, or auto-immune conditions.

Scripture highlights the difference between experiencing a healthy relationship and the effects of a broken one: "How good and pleasant it is when God's people live together in unity... there the Lord bestows his blessing, even life forevermore." (Psalm 133:1). But when we're out of harmony, the consequences are damaging: "A crushed spirit dries up the bones" (Proverbs 17:22), and "Hope deferred makes the heart sick" (Proverbs 13:12).

Barely surviving because of stress has real consequences. Beloved, God does not want that for you.

Even if it feels impossible right now, change *is* possible. Start with noticing when your body signals stress—racing heart, sweaty palms, upset stomach, or tension in your muscles. And once you notice, give yourself permission to step away from the chaos and create a pocket of safety. Breathe. Sit quietly. Reset. Maybe go for a walk. In those moments, make yourself a priority. And even outside of those moments, continue to care for your body and soul.

Make space for rest, sleep, movement, stillness, nourishing food, and nourishing friends. A massage, a warm bath, and moments in nature are great ways to release tension and restore calm.

Beloved, your body, heart, and soul were made for wholeness. Caring for yourself is not indulgent or selfish, it's lifesaving. Treat yourself with gentleness, patience, and love—and surround yourself with others who will do the same. God wants healing and restoration for you.

Prayer:

Dear Heavenly Father, thank You for guiding me toward health and healing. Give me wisdom on what my body, heart, and soul need in this season. Help me to care for myself with gentleness, patience, and love, and lead me into the rest and restoration You desire for me. Amen.

Action Step:

When you feel surrounded by chaos or notice your body becoming dysregulated (heart racing, nervous, tense), pause and take a deep breath. Slowly bring your focus to your surroundings: notice five things you see, four things you can touch, three things you can hear, two things you can smell, and one thing you can taste. This simple practice can help calm your nervous system, bring your body and mind back to safety, and help you to reset.

—Pause. Take a deep breath. What's one small step in your healing you can celebrate today?

Day 41
Navigating Triggers: When the Past Finds You

*"When anxiety was great within me,
your consolation brought me joy."*

Psalm 94:19

——*Pause. Take a few deep breaths. Now rest—and abide in Him.*——

Years ago, when my family lived in the jungles of Guyana, we attended a small village church. One service, the pastor began to raise his voice while preaching. The Guyanese can get very passionate when they preach!

Suddenly, I began to sweat—but not from the heat outside. My heart was racing, and tears started rolling down my face before I even knew why. It felt unstoppable. Embarrassed, I quickly slipped out the back and walked up and down the little jungle path nearby, sporadically crying until the service ended.

I had been triggered.

I'll be honest, the first few times this happened, I thought I was losing my mind! But over time, as the scene repeated at other services, I began to understand: My body remembered what my mind wanted to forget. Loud, angry voices in my marriage meant trouble. A loud voice meant the chaos was starting again—nights without sleep, arguments that wouldn't end, and that stomach-tying tension that flooded every fiber of my being.

Remember yesterday how we talked about how trauma gets stored in our bodies? This is one of the ways it can show up, even after we've found safety. Our bodies aren't detectives. So even when *we think* we've moved on, something from our past can still trigger us. The body can't always differentiate the past from the present—and trauma can resurface.[1]

This can look like being thrust into fight-or-flight mode when no clear threat is present, only a reminder of one. Trauma triggers can feel confusing at best—and at their worst, can be completely disorienting or even debilitating.

Many things can set them off: a sight that reminds you of something from the past, a smell, a sound, a tone of voice. Even feeling safe could trigger us—because vulnerability can make us feel like we might be exposed to more hurt.

Healing from trauma takes time. It's a process of tending to our needs, our minds, and our bodies. Dr. Cynthia Eriksson describes five R's that can be a guide as we heal. I think her simplicity here makes this easier to remember.[2]

It starts with Regulation—learning how to bring calm to our body. This could mean deep breathing, taking a walk, and definitely stepping away from the chaos. And I would add—working with someone trained in trauma recovery to walk beside you as you heal.

Then comes Reflection—noticing your thoughts. Ask yourself, "What story am I telling myself? Is it true or is it an old message from a painful moment in the past? What might I say instead that offers a gentler, more accurate perspective?"

Relationships are also an important part of healing. We weren't meant to heal alone—we are created for connection. Find people who will truly listen, pray with you, and protect your heart and story.

Rest and Respite give our minds and bodies the space they need to recover. Healing can't be rushed. It comes when we slow down, breathe, and let stillness, sleep, and the gentle rhythms of recovery do their quiet work. Sometimes healing isn't in the doing, but in giving ourselves permission to pause and rest.

And finally, Reason—or meaning—is the last R in her model for healing from trauma. We may never have all the answers for what we've endured, but we can begin to look for glimpses of purpose in it—or in our lives now. We can pray for God to weave something redemptive out of it.

Beloved, you are not weak for reacting. Remembering the pain is simply your body trying to protect you. Be gentle with yourself as you begin to find ways to feel safe again—this is tender, holy ground.

Prayer:

Dear God, help me as my body experiences the past as if it's the present. Help me slow my breathing, calm my mind, and remember You are with me—and I am safe in You. Amen.

Action Step:

Take some time and write the 5 R's of recovery from this devotional on an index card. Then keep it nearby. Use your own words so it feels personal and easy to follow. This is your journey, and these are tools to help you steady yourself when triggers arise.

–Pause. Take a deep breath. What's one small step in your healing you can celebrate today?

Day 42
Breaking the Trauma Bond

"Do not envy the wicked, do not desire their company; for their hearts plot violence, and their lips talk about making trouble."

Proverbs 24:1-2

——*Pause. Take a few deep breaths. Now rest—and abide in Him.*——

During my marriage, there were many painful arguments that would leave me crying on the floor, muffling my sobs so our son wouldn't notice. When these occurred, I would retreat to process my hurt. But often, my husband would return after cooling off—sometimes with no real intention of changing his behavior—and offer to take the family out to eat. I confused this as his way of apologizing and would agree.

Eating out was frowned on in our home, unless it was his idea, yet as a stay-at-home mom who cooked every meal from scratch, I longed for the break—and he knew it. Despite my pain, I would dry my tears, get our son ready, and go along. By the time we left, I was so exhausted from the fight and crying that I clung to his side, desperate for any hint of relief. I wanted everything to be healed in that fleeting moment of kindness and calm.

Trauma bonding is deep and confusing. A trauma bond forms when there is an emotional connection with someone who deeply harms you through demeaning words, betrayal, neglect, disrespect, invalidation, manipulation and lies, or chaotic behavior. What makes these bonds so confusing and powerful is a pattern called intermittent positive reinforcement.

Imagine this: Your spouse yells at you or ignores you for days, making you feel small or unloved. Then, suddenly, they do something kind—a compliment, a gift, a trip, or a rare moment of affection. Your heart has become so starved for affection and maybe even kindness that it can't help but cling to those moments of "goodness." Over time, your brain starts to tolerate the dysfunction just to experience those fleeting moments of relief. And when their attention is withdrawn as punishment, it can feel as consuming as withdrawal symptoms from an addiction—you'll do almost anything to get that sense of calm and affection back.

Breaking free from this cycle can feel much like overcoming an addiction—confusion, self-doubt and blame, intense longings to reconnect, fear of abandonment, loneliness, anxiety, depression, and guilt. It can even create physical side effects, such as insomnia, changes in appetite, headaches, and muscle tension.

If this sounds familiar, dear friend, please hear me: It doesn't mean you're broken. It means your heart and mind have done their very best to survive something deeply painful. It means you have a tender, hopeful heart that longs for reconciliation—but true reconciliation is only possible when real change has taken place.

Healing begins when you start to notice these patterns for what they are and take steps toward reclaiming your boundaries, your emotional and physical safety, and your joy.

Scripture reminds us, "Do not envy the wicked, do not desire their company; for their hearts plot violence, and their lips talk about making trouble" (Proverbs 24:1-2, NIV). If this describes your relationship with your husband or boyfriend, dear friend, it's important to begin working on your internal beliefs about your worth and to surround yourself with those who are steady, trustworthy, and nurturing.

Healing from trauma bonding doesn't mean you stop longing for connection—it means you begin to long for the *right kind*. The kind that reflects God's character. God's love is not based on cycles of tension and relief. It's steady. It restores dignity instead of stripping it away. It draws you close instead of pushing you away.

When you begin to anchor your worth in Him, the grip of unhealthy attachment starts to loosen. You were never meant to live on emotional crumbs. God invites you to feast on His goodness, care, and love—whether through His Word, prayer, or through safe people who honor and support you. This is how the bond breaks, not by sheer willpower, but by learning what true love and care feel like.

Prayer:

Dear God, I have experienced trauma in my marriage and my heart longs for healing and wholeness. I pray for restoration where it's possible, and for the courage to see clearly if it isn't. If not, give me the strength to take the necessary steps to protect my heart. Help me to trust that Your plans for me are good, and that You will be with me no matter what comes.

Reflection:

What would protecting your heart—with God's help—look like in this season of your life?

–Pause. Take a deep breath. What's one small step in your healing you can celebrate today?

Day 43
Moving Forward With or Without Fear

"For God has not given us a spirit of fear, but of power and of love and of a sound mind."
2 Timothy 1:7, NKJV

———*Pause. Take a few deep breaths. Now rest—and abide in Him.*———

Years ago, my family and I accepted a call to serve as missionaries in Papua New Guinea. I was thrilled at the idea, though in reality, I may have romanticized it a bit. I had read *many* missionary stories with my son, so I envisioned jungle adventures and powerful testimonies. But almost immediately after saying yes, *different* stories started flooding in.

Stories of missionaries in that area who had been harmed, some who had to flee for their lives, and just before we left, a beautiful missionary who lost his life. It felt like the whole host of hell was out to terrify me and keep me from going. Not to mention, I was just beginning to understand the devastation in my own marriage.

Still, we went forward. Thirty-two hours of flying total—most of it over endless stretches of dark ocean, filled with turbulence. We touched down briefly in Hong Kong in the middle of the night, then onto the capital airport, and finally onto the small mission plane that dropped us into our new home cradled in the highlands. My family slept *soundly* through our travels—I did not.

My anxiety had grown during our trip, and as a result, so had my need for the bathroom! I spent most of the long flight over the ocean precariously climbing over the very tall, elderly businessman beside me, his head bobbing each time I jostled him awake to rush once more to the airplane bathroom. By the time we finally arrived in the pre-dawn hours, I was sleep deprived and frazzled.

The darkness in the deep, wide valley was like nothing I had ever experienced. No streetlights, just silence and smoke rising from the piles of trash left burning in yards. The new smells, unfamiliar sights, and isolation overwhelmed me. And I shut down.

I barely left my new bedroom for weeks. While my family excitedly settled in and explored, I was paralyzed. Fear had wrapped itself around me and wouldn't let go.

Maybe you know that feeling. Maybe your world has shifted under your feet in ways you never imagined. Maybe you discovered your husband's betrayal. Maybe you're living in a home that looks normal on the outside but is filled with coercion, control, or danger. Or maybe, you're wrestling with the terrifying "what ifs" of leaving—or staying.

Fear is loud. It speaks in worst-case scenarios. It tells us we're not strong enough, we'll never make it, or that it's just better to stay quiet and stay put. But, friend, fear is a liar.

One day after weeks in bed, I got up and I got dressed. Determined to not let fear be the boss of me, I told my son we were going to the market. He looked at me stunned: "But, Mom... you don't even know how to drive on the other side of the road!"

Yep, he was right. I didn't. But I was done letting fear dictate my life. So, we went. And I only ended up on the wrong side of the road once that day (and no one died!). I celebrated. Not because I had done anything impressive, but because I had taken one step toward freedom. One step toward living life again. Yes, I had to take my fear with me, but I decided I would just have to strap it in for the ride!

God knows we will experience fear. Fear is not a flaw or a sign that we're broken—it's our body's way of keeping us safe. Fear alerts our nervous system of danger—God designed us this way. That fear helped me to be wise while we were out and about that day. But, Scripture also reminds us that a "spirit of fear" is not from God and that He empowers us with a sound mind (2 Timothy 1:7).

This doesn't mean you won't be afraid at times—you will—but it means God equips us to move forward even when we're afraid. Courage is not the absence of fear; it's moving forward in the presence of it.

You don't have to have it all figured out. Just be ready to act when you need to—whether that's reaching out for help, making a Safety Plan, speaking your truth, or simply letting yourself be real about what you're going through. God promises to meet us in our courage, even when to us it feels like fear.

Prayer:

Dear Father, You know my fears better than anyone. You know what keeps me awake at night. You also know the beginning from the end. Help me to trust that You will protect me and my children and that You desire for us to live in safety and wholeness. Please help me to begin taking the steps toward safety and healing, and hold me and my fears as I do. Amen.

Reflection:

What are you fearful of—something in your marriage, a truth you don't want to see, or your safety? Write down your fears, fill out the Safety Plan if you haven't already, and begin to move toward protection, peace, and freedom.

—Pause. Take a deep breath. What's one small step in your healing you can celebrate today?

Day 44
You Can Love and Still Leave

"Be strong and courageous. Do not be afraid or terrified because of them, for the Lord your God goes with you; He will never leave you nor forsake you."

Deuteronomy 31:6

———Pause. Take a few deep breaths. Now rest—and abide in Him.———

Think of a marriage like a dance. In order for a dance to be coordinated and beautiful, each person must move in rhythm with the other. When that stops, you end up with a slightly uncoordinated dance—or, worse, a painful series of moves where one person is trampled. Imagine: broken limbs, bruised toes, and growing fear—think *mosh pit*, not waltz.

At the start, I outlined four types of marriages: the Uncoordinated, the Unfulfilling, the Undiagnosed or Untreated, and the Unsafe or Unsustainable. The last category often includes betrayal, addiction, infidelity, abandonment, and abuse—destructive behaviors that repeat and erode safety and well-being. This is the category where the conversation of separation or divorce often arises—and rightfully so.

If these behaviors are ongoing—or even if they're not, but they're destructive enough to harm you or your children—then, dear friend, we need to have a heart to heart.

Sometimes when you "change the dance" in your relationship, your spouse may respond with true repentance (refer to day 36 for signs). But this depends solely on him being responsible for his actions, and not you enabling his sin, staying silent, or trying to fix him. You are *only* responsible for your actions and responses—*not* his.

Setting healthy boundaries is one way to change the dance and *potentially* the outcome. Yet, sometimes, nothing changes. You may still find yourself in a chaotic mosh pit, never knowing when his next emotional or physical blow will come. Protecting your sanity and safety by separating or divorcing is not betrayal or sin—it's biblical wisdom.

Many women struggle to leave because they believe it goes against God, or because their husband claims to be a Christian who prays, so surely God will change him. Beloved, God never forces anyone to change; your husband has to *want* to change.

You may see him praying daily and feel even more confused about why nothing is changing. Scripture is clear: Husbands must be considerate, respectful, and gentle with their wives, *"so that nothing will hinder [their] prayers"* (1 Peter 3:7). According to God, abusive or deceptive behavior nullifies his prayers.

Your husband may claim to be a Christian, but if he continues to abuse, betray, or emotionally abandon you, he is *not* a true believer—because if he were, he would truly repent and turn from his ways. The Bible warns us of wolves in sheep's clothing and people whose hearts aren't pure (Matthew 7:15, Galatians 5:19-21). Jesus says, "Not everyone who says to me, 'Lord, Lord,' will enter the kingdom of heaven" (Matthew 7:20-23). And Ephesians 5:3-7 lists many wicked behaviors God abhors, and then concludes with this: "Therefore do not be partners with them."

God knows that staying in such a home can make you and your children lose hope or adopt harmful coping behaviors yourselves.

He also knows that enabling your husband's sin doesn't help him; staying without consequences can signal that his behavior is condoned and can continue unchecked.

Boundaries, counseling, and speaking your truth can lead to true repentance and restore the marriage—but when that doesn't happen, leaving *is* the safest, wisest, and healthiest choice. Make safety your top priority and seek support from trusted people or professionals. Even God set boundaries with those He loved. You can still love your husband and leave.

God does not call you to stay where you—or your children—are harmed. Staying in abuse teaches them that safety doesn't matter—and that pain can echo across generations. God loves you *all* too much for that.

Prayer:

Dear Father, I have felt paralyzed and stuck, not knowing what to do. I need Your wisdom to protect my safety—even if Your guidance doesn't sound like what my pastor, my church, my family, or even my counselor has told me. Surround me with Your peace, guide my steps, and help me trust that choosing safety is right. Amen.

Reflection:

Reflect on whether you truly feel emotionally, spiritually, or physically safe in your marriage. Emotional safety looks like not feeling hopeless, fearful, or suicidal because of the stress in your marriage. For guidance on determining if it's wise to stay, refer back to day 36 to see if your husband shows signs of true repentance and lasting change.

While there may be situations where you need to remain temporarily—for example, until you can secure housing, gather resources, or stabilize financially—your immediate safety should always come first. If there is any threat of harm, it's safest to leave as soon as possible and seek help.

For signs that your marriage has the potential for increased danger, review the D.A.N.G.E.R. checklist at the end of this devotional. And if you're unsure or feel unsafe, complete the Safety Plan (link provided) in the back of the book and keep it stored discreetly.

–Pause. Take a deep breath. What's one small step in your healing you–
can celebrate today?

Day 45
When the System Fails, God Does Not

"Speak up for those who cannot speak for themselves."
Proverbs 31:8-9

——*Pause. Take a few deep breaths. Now rest—and abide in Him.*——

Dear sister, today I want to speak with you as one mother to another. One of the hardest things to walk through as a mother is deeply desiring to protect our little ones from harm and feeling like we're failing. It can be absolutely gut wrenching.

Yet sometimes, despite our very best efforts, it's out of our hands. There may be times when the system fails our children and doesn't keep them safe. In those moments, God invites us to cling tightly to His hand.

We want justice to do what justice *should* do—keep our children out of harm's way and far from abuse. Yet those in charge sometimes choose to see it differently, believing that contact with an abusive parent is better than no contact at all. Justifying that having both parents, even if one is abusive, is always the better route.

So, they leave our children defenseless against the very harm we've been so desperately trying to protect them from. I'm certain this grieves God's heart.

God would never place our children in harm's way. His Word tells us so in Matthew 18:6, Mark 9:42, and in Luke 17:2. I believe He feels so strongly about this that He placed these warnings about not causing any little one to stumble in *three* of the Gospels.

Yet, in this broken world, we, and sadly our children, will face tribulation. Not because God isn't good and just, and not because He caused it, but because human beings with free will sometimes choose wrongly and do things unjustly.

If this is where you find yourself, I want to share with you a bit more of the heart of our Father today. Because, despite others doing wrong and not defending our little ones, God longs to. And He often uses protective mothers to stand in the breach between good and evil.

He tells us in Proverbs 31:8-9 (NLT) to "speak up for those who cannot speak for themselves; ensure justice for those being crushed. Yes, speak up for the poor and helpless, and see that they get justice." This includes advocating within the system and using every resource available to seek your children's safety, while trusting God to guide you.

And He calls us to do so wisely: "Be wise as serpents and harmless as doves" (Matthew 10:16, NKJV). Why? Because the enemy of souls is deceptive. If we lash out in anger or pain, we risk letting the evil around us seep into our own souls—and teach our children the same. But when we lean into God's strength, then we are truly strong for the fight (2 Corinthians 12:9-10).

Listen to how Scripture describes the way God shepherds those He loves in Isaiah 40:11 (NLT, emphasis added): "He will feed his flock like a shepherd. He will carry the lambs in his arms, holding them close to his heart. He will gently lead the *mother* sheep *with their young*."

He guides us as we're able, gently. Yes, we are called to stand up for our little (and not so little) ones and protect them, but we also need to allow God to carry us when we're weary from the battle.

Dear sweet momma, I understand what it feels like to be wearied from the battle at home. So, I want to encourage you to take one small step today: Tell your Heavenly Father your needs and your children's needs. He is there to hold you *and* to guide you and your children. Then with wisdom, keep advocating and staying proactive on their behalf. He is with you, He is for you, and He will hold you as you fight for their safety.

Prayer:

Dear Heavenly Father, I never imagined that I would have to protect my children from the very person who was meant to love them. Hold me in the grief that comes with this and grant me wisdom to be wise as a serpent yet gentle as a dove as I navigate keeping my children safe. Amen.

Reflection/Action Steps:

It is wise to begin keeping a written record of each incident (with the date) while the details are fresh, and save any texts, emails, voicemails, medical reports, or witness statements. Keep these in a safe, private place. These records can help create a paper trail if legal action becomes necessary. Remember, you are not being disloyal—you are protecting your flock. God calls you to be "wise as a serpent and harmless as a dove."

If any violence or sexual abuse occurs, call the police right away—don't wait to assess whether it's "bad enough." Showing your children that abuse is never acceptable teaches them truth, courage, and safety. Keep a copy of your police report; it may be needed for court proceedings or a custody case.

–Pause. Take a deep breath. What's one small step in your healing you can celebrate today?

Day 46

Protecting Your Little (and Not So Little) Ones

"He tends his flock like a shepherd: He gathers the lambs in his arms and carries them close to his heart."
Isaiah 40:11, NLT

——*Pause. Take a few deep breaths. Now rest—and abide in Him.*——

In my own story—and in the stories of many women I've worked with since—we found ourselves standing in the gap between our husband's harsh, controlling, or abusive behaviors and a bewildered child. Even when we offered firm, loving guidance and gentle corrections, the backlash became harsher. They instilled fear, as we worked to create safety. Many times, the reasons for extreme punishment were painfully arbitrary—like refusing to eat food that made the child feel sick or wanting to wear a skirt that came just slightly above the knees.

When we tried to protect our children from unkindness or extreme, rigid control, it was seen as disrespect and fueled resentment. Our main job turned into defending our children's hearts when our husbands couldn't recognize that discipline had tipped into harm or abuse. Simply standing up for a hurting and discouraged child could be labeled as defiance, leaving both mother and child exhausted and confused.

In my son's younger years, I couldn't be the mom I longed to be. I remember the weary days of trying to make sense of it all. Some days, my body gave out from the tension or arguments, often over parenting or small mistakes, and I'd collapse into a deep sleep just to escape for a while. Most days my energy went into managing dysfunction instead of making memories with my son. I had to grieve this loss as I began to heal. My son says that I did the best I could—and I did—but it was still a loss for both of us.

When he became a pre-teen, I finally found the strength to separate and began to see more clearly what we had lived through. Since then, God has graciously brought healing to both of us. I've never shied away from telling him how sorry I am that he had to grow up in such confusion.

Though I didn't cause the abuse, I want him to know how deeply I grieve the parts of his childhood that were lost because of it. Even now, I try to remember all that he's endured, and when *I* fall short, to apologize and make real amends. I'm far from perfect, but I'm more aware of what even small wounds can do to a child's heart—whether young or old—so I keep striving to rise higher and be the best mother I can be for him.

Friend, if this is your story, it doesn't make you a bad mother, either. It makes you a mom who's been carrying a heavy load while learning to set boundaries and walk in truth. One quote that helped me came from Maya Angelou, who said, "When we know better, we do better."

You may just be awakening to all that's truly happening; be sure to give yourself grace. Your story may look different—you may be the one carrying the full weight of being the disciplinarian alone. That same grace applies if you snap or speak to your children in frustration—sincere apologies and genuine efforts to do better go further than you think.

Our children need to hear, often, that the tension in the home is not their fault, and that we're working to protect them and to get help. I believe this bears repeating from yesterday's devotional—God is tender with our children—and with us as weary moms: "He will feed his flock like a shepherd. He will carry the lambs in his arms, holding them close to his heart. He will gently lead the mother sheep with their young" (Isaiah 40:11, NLT)

What a comfort to know that God not only carries our children close to His heart, but also gently leads us as moms. He calls us to protect and guide our little ones, to honor their tender hearts, and to model a life lived in truth and love. And He also calls us to extend that same grace to ourselves.

You are taking the right steps now. You are showing your children what courage, dignity, and grace look like in real life. You're doing a good work, momma. Don't lose heart, God is there for you—lean on His strength.

Prayer:

Dear Father, my husband hasn't treated our children as You would. Sometimes he is too harsh and other times far too permissive, leaving me to protect my children from the confusion it all creates. Give me wisdom, patience, and strength to guide them with love, and help me trust You to lift me up when I'm weary. Amen.

Reflection:

In the Resource section of this devotional, you'll find more parenting help as you navigate supporting your children. Take a moment to reflect on the steps you can take to help protect their hearts while your husband seeks help or as you make plans to get to safety.

*On a sensitive note: Abuse and stress can begin to fracture your ability to parent safely. If you ever find yourself feeling overwhelmed to the point where you might lose control, hit, or hurt your child, please seek help immediately—for your sake and for your child's safety. Reaching out is a sign of strength, not failure.

–Pause. Take a deep breath. What's one small step in your healing you can celebrate today?

Day 47
Strengthening Your Support System

"Two are better than one, because they have a good return for their labor: If either of them falls down, one can help the other up."

Ecclesiastes 4:9-10

———*Pause. Take a few deep breaths. Now rest—and abide in Him.*———

I remember years ago when I was just awakening to what was really happening in my marriage, I felt so alone and isolated. My family had moved so often that I never put strong roots down anywhere. But I needed support—my marriage felt confusing, heavy, and lonely.

At first, my husband and I were talking with ministry leaders who were "peer counseling" us. This was not wise; in fact, it was harmful. Eventually, I found a counselor of my own. She was life giving. She helped me name what I was experiencing. I'll forever be grateful for her. She is one of the reasons I went back to get my degree in counseling—I knew there was a desperate need for more trauma- and abuse-informed professionals.

I also found an online support group, which I attended faithfully for close to a year. I would often put in my earbuds while driving my kiddo to town to listen in, telling him, "Mom has a meeting she can't miss." Those meetings became another lifeline, a safe space where I could breathe and be understood.

Slowly, I began to test my existing circle of friends to see who I could trust with the hard truth about my marriage. I quickly realized that some people weren't safe to share with—not because they were bad, but because their guidance or neutrality left me more confused, hopeless, or wounded.

I learned that the people who insisted on "hearing both sides" had, by default, made themselves unsafe to connect with. A safe person doesn't weigh both perspectives when one partner is abusive; they automatically seek to protect your heart and care for you. For my emotional safety, I had to distance myself from those who couldn't do that—and grieve those losses.

But then there were what I can only call angels in disguise. A sweet pastor who offered to help my son and me find a place of safety and rest. My closest friends, who never left my side, were my fierce truth-tellers. Family who, without hesitation, stepped in to support us. The ladies in my support groups. As I prayed for help, God provided. But I had to be willing to let some people go and allow others to come close.

I understand how hard it can be to open up to others. My family served in ministry and missions for years, and while we were busy planting a new church, my marriage was falling apart. Shame kept me silent. You, too, may feel ashamed to share what's happening because of your husband's position or reputation, or for fear of what others might think, the sense that your marriage isn't "as bad" as others, or because you've been taught that marital issues should be kept private. But, sweet friend, you need people who can bear witness to your pain and help support you in your healing—no matter the outcome of your marriage.

Sweet friend, if you are in the middle of a hard season, please know: You don't have to go it alone. In fact, you shouldn't. There are safe people who can encourage you and listen without judgment. Seek these people and don't be afraid to let others go if you need to. Pray for God to provide the lifelines you need, and don't be afraid to open your heart to receive them.

Prayer:

Dear Father, help me to not be afraid to reach out for help. Please send people who are trauma- and abuse-informed to help me find the answers I've been seeking. And give me the wisdom to know who I can trust. Amen.

Reflection:

Who can you trust to hold your story with care and confidentiality? Is it time to reach out to an abuse-informed counselor, coach, or support group so you don't have to carry this alone?

–Pause. Take a deep breath. What's one small step in your healing you can celebrate today?

Day 48
God Can Handle Your Hard Questions

"Yet I will rejoice in the Lord, I will be joyful in God my Savior."
Habakkuk 3:18

——*Pause. Take a few deep breaths. Now rest—and abide in Him.*——

Habakkuk lived during a time in history when all he could see was turmoil in his world. There were imminent hostile takeovers happening in the powers that be and Habakkuk was frustrated because he felt like God was silent in the midst of it all.

What I love about Habakkuk is he wasn't afraid to ask the hard questions. Why do the wicked seem to win, while those who are just trying to do right are being crushed? He saw injustice, suffering, and evil thriving—and couldn't help but wonder where God was in all of it.

If I'm honest, I've asked these same questions. It can be tempting to give up asking God for deliverance from something when it seems like He is a million miles away. But I love Habakkuk's continual childlike faith. Even though things were beyond hard for him, he continued to give his heavy heart to God. He didn't cut the cord of connection. But he also didn't hold back his very real, tough questions about God's goodness either. And you know what? God was (and is) big enough to handle these kinds of prayers.

God didn't give Habakkuk all the answers right away, but He listened to each one and responded with mercy and wisdom. He reminded him there's a bigger picture—one he couldn't see yet. God told Habakkuk to trust, even when things were hard, because ultimately, His justice would prevail (Habakkuk 2:2-3).

The same is true for you and me: Life can absolutely be unfair, painful, even utterly confusing at times, but we're invited to trust God—even if we don't understand what He is doing.

Habakkuk's ultimate response is deep. He says, even if every single means of sustenance fails (no fruit trees or gardens bear food, no meat to eat), and I am literally destitute, "Yet I will rejoice in the Lord, I will be joyful in God my Savior." He goes on to say: "The Sovereign Lord is my strength; he makes my feet like the feet of a deer, he enables me to tread on the heights" (Habakkuk 3:17-19).

Let that sink in for a minute. That's powerful. Praise even when everything seems broken.

Faith when fear wants to take over. And trust, when nothing, even God, seems trustworthy.

God heard his prayers and delivered him.

Hold on to Him, sweet friend. Even when the sky seems to be falling, God hasn't left you. He always hears your prayers, even if His "response" feels slow, or He calls you to take a step that feels unsteady.

He will always be beside you to catch you; just don't cut that cord of connection. Keep the lines open and be real with Him; He can handle it.

Prayer:

Dear God, right now my life also feels like it is experiencing a hostile takeover. Help me to trust You even when I can't understand. I'm frustrated, Lord—tired of waiting, tired of watching things fall apart. But like Habakkuk, I'm still coming to You. Meet me here in my questions, and help me to believe You're at work, even when I can't see it. Amen.

Reflection:

What deep and honest questions are you carrying right now? Don't be afraid to bring them to God; He isn't afraid of your doubts or your pain. He can hold it all with tenderness.

—Pause. Take a deep breath. What's one small step in your healing you can celebrate today?

Day 49
Feelings Aren't Failure

"A time to heal; A time to break down, And a time to build up; A time to weep, And a time to laugh; A time to mourn, And a time to dance."

Ecclesiastes 3:1-8

——*Pause. Take a few deep breaths. Now rest—and abide in Him.*——

Dear friend, have you ever felt like you were sinning for feeling strong emotions toward another person? Maybe you've been stuck in anger that won't fade, or sadness that lingers longer than you think it should.

We often hear sermons about "not holding on to anger," or how "God gives us joy, so we shouldn't feel sad." Sometimes even, "if we truly trusted God, we would never worry."

When emotions are attached to moral meaning, it's easy to start moralizing our feelings. *I can't stop being anxious, so I must not have enough faith.* Or, *I feel sad, so maybe I'm not walking closely enough with God.*

But what if that's not how God sees our emotions?

Scripture tells us we are made in God's image—and Jesus, who perfectly represented His image, wept, rejoiced, and even felt anger. Emotions aren't flaws to fix; they're connections to God's own heart.

Scripture says, "To everything *there is a season*, a time for every purpose under heaven—a time to heal, to mourn, to embrace" (emphasis added). Our emotions are like the seasons; they have a time and a purpose, too.

Think of your emotions like the weather. They can shift and change; each season has a purpose. We wouldn't pretend it's sunny out when it's storming—we would grab an umbrella and respond wisely. In the same way your feelings are not moral failures, they're indicators.

Just like pain sensors tell our bodies something is wrong when we touch a hot stove, emotions tell our hearts something needs attention. We want our pain sensors to alert us if something can harm us, so we can protect ourselves. Emotions are signals meant to protect, to guide, and to help us to heal.

Yet, when we've lived through control, chaos, or abuse, we may have learned to silence or distrust our feelings. Maybe we were even told we were "too sensitive" or "too emotional." So, we tried to get *over* our feelings by suppressing, numbing, denying, or ignoring them. But what if healing doesn't mean "getting over" our feelings, but rather learning to listen to them wisely?

Sometimes, feelings do ease when we give them space to be felt—but other times, they linger because there's something in our lives that still needs healing. That doesn't make you weak or faithless; it just means your heart is alerting you to something that still needs care.

Our emotions aren't meant to steer our ship, but they are meant to be a part of our navigational system. When anger arises, it may be signaling that our boundary has been crossed. When sadness lingers, it's inviting us to finish grieving what's been lost. Or when fears shows up, it could be cautioning us to slow down or pay attention.

But sometimes what we don't realize is that we keep circling the same emotional waters because we haven't acted on what the emotion was trying to tell us. We wonder why we can't stop feeling bitter—yet we keep replaying the story of the wrong done to us or stay close to the very person who keeps burning us, which keeps the story alive.

It's like touching a hot stove and then praying the pain will go away, while keeping our hand on the burner. When we ruminate on what hurt us but don't set boundaries or create distance, we give that person space to live rent-free in our minds—and the pain keeps repeating itself.

We don't have to let emotions take control, but we also don't have to throw them overboard. We can sit with them, name them, understand what they're trying to teach us—and then, little by little, let God's Spirit steer us toward peace, safety, and wisdom.

Because your emotions, beloved, are not the enemy. They serve a purpose in your healing and need to be given space to do their work.

Prayer:

Dear Father, help me to see that my emotions are not the enemy. If I'm still feeling deep pain, remind me that it may be because I'm still in a place where I'm being wounded. Please lead me to emotional and physical safety so I can better regulate my emotions and allow my heart to heal. Amen.

Reflection:

Are you struggling with any particular emotion right now? If so, take a moment to name it. What might it be trying to show you? What does this feeling point to that you deeply want or value?

—Pause. Take a deep breath. What's one small step in your healing you– can celebrate today?

Day 50

Anger is Not a Sin

"Be angry, and do not sin."
Psalm 4:4, NKJV

───*Pause. Take a few deep breaths. Now rest—and abide in Him.*───

Anger is a God-given emotion—and beloved, you may feel downright angry right now. Rightfully so.

Anger is that emotion that simmers in your soul at the injustice of what has happened to you. Anger can feel messy, but harnessed, it can be productive. It's one of the most energizing emotions God has given us. It can drive us to advocate for justice, move toward safety, or make needed changes in our lives.

But maybe your anger has been stifled and even used against you by the very one creating the chaos in your life. Often, an abusive or dishonest person does this to keep the focus on your reactions *instead* of their behaviors. This keeps *you* feeling guilty for expressing anger, instead of holding them accountable for hurting you. Suddenly you're repenting of your frustration, instead of protecting yourself against their sin.

Beloved, don't let their deflection confuse you—God understands your anger after being wronged.

God expresses His own anger many times in Scripture (Romans 1:18, Psalm 7:11, Romans 2:5), often to protect His people from injustice or from committing it against Him or each other. When God acts in anger, it's out of love, not because He delights in destruction (Isaiah 28:21). His anger is righteous, and since we're made in His image, it's natural that we, too, will feel anger against injustice. He just doesn't want it to fester in our hearts and turn into bitterness or a desire for revenge (Hebrews 12:15).

To understand this more fully, it's helpful to understand that there are two kinds of anger. One is constructive anger, which we see in Psalm 4:4, when God said, "Be angry, and do not sin." God was telling David he had every right to be angry at the harm done to him, but not to act in a destructive way in return.

The second kind, destructive anger, is the kind that leads to harmful actions. When your husband hits you, yells at you, curses at you, deeply neglects you, or betrays you, these are acts of destructive anger. These are sins God does *not* approve of. Constructive anger, on the other hand, is what you naturally feel in *response* to these things.

Anger itself is a secondary emotion. There's always something more fragile under it.

So, beneath the anger, you may feel criticized, numb, violated—or have feelings of fear, indignation, or humiliation. Anger is your mind grappling with the truth that what's happening is deeply wrong, when you don't yet know how to address it. It's the strong emotion God has given us to express the vulnerable emotions we don't yet know how to express.

Anger is often called an iceberg emotion. On the surface we see anger. It's visible like the tip of the iceberg—but deep beneath the surface lingers the depth of your pain. It's where the most wounded and fragile parts of your story live. This is where you find your hurt over being stifled, controlled, silenced, or deeply betrayed by your husband. This is where the parts of you live that longed to be loved but instead were neglected.

Beloved, if you're being abused or betrayed, you have *every* right to feel angry. God is angry about it, too. But He wants that anger to motivate you to seek healing and protection, not revenge.

Remember: Vengeance belongs to God, but *choice* belongs to you. You don't have to allow abusive behaviors to keep destroying your life.

Sweet friend, pray—not to keep things as they are, but to place your husband in God's hands for justice while taking steps to protect yourself and reclaim your peace. Yes, you can still love your husband but hate the injustice and the sin. God does.

You are being called to rise higher. Allow your anger to motivate you toward healing and restoration—emotionally, physically, and spiritually. Let God in to restore what's been lost. He wants to be your defender, because You are that precious to Him.

Prayer:

Dear Heavenly Father, I feel the weight of anger, hurt, and fear from all I've endured. Please help me to use these emotions to set boundaries and to protect myself and my children. Help me to rise higher in Your strength. Guide me to make wise choices and restore what has been lost. Please be my refuge as I actively work on making my home a place of peace and healing. Amen.

Reflection:

How can you allow your anger to motivate you to move toward emotional, physical, and spiritual restoration and safety? Are there boundaries you need to set, conversations you need to have, or space you need to create to ensure you and your children are safe?

—Pause. Take a deep breath. What's one small step in your healing you– can celebrate today?

Day 51
Releasing Bitterness

"See to it that no one falls short of the grace of God and that no bitter root grows up to cause trouble and defile many."
Hebrews 12:15

——*Pause. Take a few deep breaths. Now rest—and abide in Him.*——

I learned early in my marriage that if I expressed being hurt by my husband's behavior, he would either yell louder or make it clear through his looks or words that I wasn't allowed to be upset. So, I began to suppress my feelings.

I wanted to be a godly wife, and submission and *suppression* aligned with what I was hearing in sermons, at retreats, and even in conversations with ministry leaders who counseled couples. So, I tried to submit more and silence any hint of hurt or frustration.

But, a few years into my marriage, something inside me swelled. I couldn't stay silent anymore when my husband talked down or yelled at my son or me. I fought back. If he raised his voice, I did, too. But it didn't help.

I felt myself growing angry and bitter. I could sense my heart becoming dark and ugly, and eventually hopelessness took root, pushing me into complete emotional shutdown.

During that season, I realized my relationship with the Lord was at stake. I had become someone I no longer recognized. For years, I had felt overwhelmed, but now I was also angry at life and, at times, even at God for not stopping the abuse. Deep down, though, I knew God didn't want me to allow that anger to fester.

Slowly, Scripture began speaking into my hurting places. In 2 Corinthians 3:18, God shares this principle: By beholding, we become changed. If we behold Christ-like behavior, we naturally begin to change in Christ-like ways. This is the ideal in marriage: Two sinners, who admittedly aren't perfect, but are still trying to out-serve one another to reflect Christ's love.

But in unsafe and unsustainable marriages, the opposite happens. Survivors are forced to behold behavior that is anything but Christ-like. In that environment, it becomes harder and harder to rise above the toxicity and dysfunction. And soon, our own hearts grow cold.

For me, change began when I realized *I* had a part in the cycles that kept repeating in our marriage. I was also repeating my own familiar dysfunction. I continued avoiding the boundaries I desperately needed for emotional safety. I was so conflict-avoidant that I ran from the hard conversations, afraid of upsetting anyone. Yet I blamed God, as though it was *His fault* for not making it all stop.

Eventually, I had to face the hard truth: God never forces anyone to do anything. It was my husband's free will to seek help—or not. *And* it was my free will to decide what to do if he didn't.

God was not at fault for his choices, nor for my lack of boundaries. When I took responsibility for what was mine to own, it helped release the bitterness I was carrying. I realized I wasn't trapped; I *could* choose to leave—it wasn't God holding me there.

What kept me in the abuse were other people misusing Scripture, my own misunderstandings about how God views divorce, and the deep shame I carried, thinking I would be a "failure" if I walked away. But none of that was God either.

Once I finally surrendered my bitterness to God and faced the reality of what was happening in my marriage, I found Him waiting for me. He had never left.

It was there, in that place of honesty, that He began teaching me how to move forward—by speaking my truth in love, and learning how to value both myself and my marriage enough not to allow the abuse to continue. God knows that if we allow anger to settle down into our souls, it will spring up as bitterness and can keep us from connecting with *anyone* in a healthy way (Hebrews 12:15).

Dear friend, I don't know your situation, but I do know this: Letting go of the toxicity in your heart can make room for God's peace—whether or not your marriage is healed. And that's truly the only thing we have control of—ourselves.

Prayer:

Dear God, please search my heart and find any root of bitterness within me. Help me to uproot it so I can live in Your peace. Guide me to make healthy choices that protect my heart, mind, and sanity, so I no longer feel overwhelmed by hopelessness or anger. Amen.

Reflection:

Where might bitterness or anger still be taking root in your heart? What small steps can you take to protect your peace and honor the life God has given you?

–Pause. Take a deep breath. What's one small step in your healing you can celebrate today?

Day 52

Reacting is Not Abuse

*"I do not understand what I do.
For what I want to do I do not do, but what I hate I do."*
Romans 7:15

———*Pause. Take a few deep breaths. Now rest—and abide in Him.*———

Donna came to see me week after week, exhausted and bedraggled from the chaos at home. Then one day, something shifted. She showed up with a different countenance—still tired, but something was different.

"I snapped," she said. "He was getting emphatic and pushing his way again. I just couldn't take it anymore—and I snapped."

She proceeded to share how she had angrily swiped a vase off the table nearby where they were arguing. She recounted that it felt like her frustration from being pressured and belittled for the umpteenth time had finally exploded. Then she began to cry.

As I held space for the heavy shame she had been carrying, I grieved with her that she ever had to get to that place. I had been there before. I didn't judge her or think that suddenly she had become the abuser. But she did.

Then the question came: "How can I hold him accountable for his actions, when I'm just as bad?" Then more tears, more holding space for this hard place in her journey.

Dear friend, if you've been in Donna's shoes, you, too, may wonder at times if *you're* abusive also. There's a name for this—several, actually. One term used is *reactive abuse*, though I believe more accurate terms might be *self-defense*, *reactive survival mechanism*, or *trauma response*. Whatever the names, most of these terms carry the same sentiment for survivors of abuse.

They mean that victims of abuse eventually react to being abused—because they're human. We weren't made to digest a daily ration of poison and stay poised. We have nervous systems that beg to be treated with fairness and kindness. And when they're not, they wear out. Donna's had worn out.

Friend, if this is you, it does not mean you've suddenly become the abuser. Even if your husband tries to twist it around and place the blame on you. That's DARVO in action, not truth.

However, if you've reached this place, it's a very clear sign you need to move toward peace apart from the cycles so your nervous system can rest. This can become a slippery slope toward escalation, burn out, and desperation—or it can be the beginning of something brave and healing.

God understands why you would feel angry because there are times when anger is justified. He tells us so: "Be angry, and do not sin" (Ephesians 4:26, NKJV).

God knows we will feel anger and a sense of injustice when we're wronged. But I believe the second part of that verse is His way of saying don't stay in the cycles. Don't allow anyone's behavior to become your behavior. Protect your own soul.

Peace isn't found in silence or suppression—it's found away from the chaos. It's found in truth and safety, and in the steady love of God, who has seen every bruise, every tear, and every longing of your heart.

Prayer:

Dear God, please help me recognize what I'm feeling when I'm provoked. Teach me how to set healthy boundaries and step away from the arguments. You see the pain I'm carrying, and the moments when I've reacted out of deep hurt. Thank You for understanding the anger and confusion that comes from being betrayed and mistreated. And please lead me to still waters where my soul can rest and heal in Your love. Amen.

Reflection:

Think about how your body and heart respond when you're in conflict. Are there warning signs that your soul is weary or that your nervous system needs rest? What is one small step you could take today to create a safe space for peace—physically, emotionally, or spiritually?

–Pause. Take a deep breath. What's one small step in your healing you– can celebrate today?

Day 53
Trauma and Perfectionism

*"Come to me, all who labor and are heavy laden,
and I will give you rest."*

Matthew 11:28, ESV

——*Pause. Take a few deep breaths. Now rest—and abide in Him.*——

When God created man and woman, He placed them in a garden. Everything was perfect. Their sustenance, their rest, their work—every need was met. They relied on what God provided. There was harmony and peace.

But then, they chose to go a different way and start doing things without following God's wisdom, and disharmony entered their hearts.

It's the same for us. When we rely on God's ways and rest in Him, our inner world can be at peace. But when we start picking up burdens that aren't ours to carry or doing things that are outside of His wisdom—that's when the uneasiness creeps in.

When our world starts spinning out of control, it's natural to want to take the reins and fix things so we can make life "safe again." And while safety *is* what we're seeking, we often go about it the wrong way.

Trauma, pain, and heartache can leave us chasing perfection as a way to feel safe and be in control—because internally we feel out of control.

But true peace begins not in controlling everything around us, but in surrender to the One who sees our frightened hearts and understands why we're grasping so hard. It comes by focusing on the things that are actually in our control and releasing those that aren't—including other people. It comes by realizing God is calling us to progress—not our own perfection.

If you're reading this and thinking, "I can't keep going with everything God is asking of me" pause for a moment and ask yourself: "Is this truly His voice—or someone else's expectations?" Or is it your own expectations?

After abuse, it's easy to mistake the echoes of others' rules, religious demands, or shame for the voice of God. Some of us have been told that divorce is a sin, so we stay in unsafe marriages believing we *must* endure. Others have felt the pressure in their churches or social circles, calling them to serve more, do more, and to be the "perfect Christian on the outside" while quietly dying on the inside. But, friend, God's voice doesn't force you, exhaust you, or guilt you. His voice speaks truth and allows *you* the freedom to choose.

You may think God expects complete perfection from you—but, dear friend, He doesn't. He wouldn't tell us that all have sinned if we could be perfect on our own accord (Romans 3:23).

He doesn't look down at a baby just learning to crawl and scowl, "Why aren't you running yet?" Nor does he expect a young child to reason like an adult. God sees them as perfect for the stage of life they're in.

It's the same with you and me. God doesn't expect us to run when we're exhausted by pain and trauma. It's *His* perfection—not ours—that steadies us. *His* grace is sufficient, and *His* strength is made perfect *in our weakness*.

Sweet friend, if you're trying to do everything on your own, remember it's not by might, nor by power, but by His Holy Spirit that the world was formed—and by that same Spirit, He can bring peace and order to your world, too. But, you have to place your burdens in His hands and stop grasping them in yours.

I know how scary it can feel to loosen your grip—but I promise, His grip is far stronger than yours. He will not let you go.

Healing starts when we realize it's not our perfection but *His* that matters.

Prayer:

Dear God, help me to see what or who I'm holding on to tightly that You never asked me to carry, and help me to release it or them into Your hands. Amen.

Reflection:

Take a moment and reflect: Where are you striving today? What are you carrying that's not yours to carry? What or *who* are you trying to fix in your own strength, knowing deep down that it's only His strength that brings true healing?

–Pause. Take a deep breath. What's one small step in your healing you– can celebrate today?

Day 54
You're Not Failing—You're Surviving

"And He said to me, 'My grace is sufficient for you, for My strength is made perfect in weakness.'"
2 Corinthians 12:9, NKJV

———*Pause. Take a few deep breaths. Now rest—and abide in Him.*———

Years ago, we lived in a small town which was about two hours to the nearest big city, so we'd make the trip semi-frequently for special groceries, clothing, or if we needed something from one of the larger stores.

The days we traveled seemed to drag on. I'd embark on my shopping already worn out from the dysfunction in our home. Inevitably, I'd pile on other errands, which meant we'd return home late at night. Some nights I found myself picking up fast food or a protein smoothie on our return drive.

Both fast food and expensive drinks were frowned on in our home, unless it was a "special occasion." I knew bringing either home could trigger passive-aggressive comments—or escalate into full-blown arguments. Even finding a wrapper or a bottle in the car could spark a lecture that kept me awake until the wee hours about how unhealthy fast food was or how expensive that bottled drink had been.

I felt like a child being scolded by a parent—not an equal partner with the agency to decide what was best for my own body, or even an intelligent mother who knew how to care for her child. I was a grown woman who cooked wholesome meals most every day, and once in a blue moon, I needed a break. But it was treated like a sin.

So, I started stopping at the last gas station about five miles before arriving home to throw away our fast-food wrappers. My son knew the drill and was quick to notice if I forgot. "Mom, we have to throw our wrappers away!" he'd say.

I'm not telling you this because I'm proud of it. It started innocently, without me even realizing it was becoming a habit—but when I did notice the pattern, it brought deep shame. I felt awful, like I was being sneaky and teaching my son to hide things. In reality, it was a survival mechanism—a way to protect myself *and my son* from unnecessary conflict.

Eventually, as I grew stronger, I spoke up. "There *will* be times when I purchase fast food because I simply don't have time to make a picnic." It didn't always go smoothly—it could still spark arguments—but I learned to be kindly firm, set boundaries, and walk away when needed.

Sometimes you can speak your truth, and other times, the safest thing you can do is quietly protect yourself, because speaking up could put you in harm's way. Honoring the coping mechanisms that keep your children from witnessing escalation or aggression until you're truly safe is wisdom, not weakness.

Here's what I want you to hear: Survival doesn't mean failure. Coping mechanisms, even the ones we later feel embarrassed about, are signs we're navigating life in an unhealthy or unsafe environment. You're not failing for protecting yourself.

Other times, when you notice habits that *aren't* about safety, that's an opportunity—first, to show yourself grace, and second, to course correct.

No matter what anyone tells you, *no one* has ever navigated chaos and dysfunction perfectly. Progress, not perfection, is what we're seeking here.

So please, dear friend, have grace on yourself. If there are times you aren't showing up as your best self, that's OK. You're taking brave steps by showing up here. God sees your effort and honors it. And His grace is sufficient in our weakness (2 Corinthians 12:9)

Prayer:

Dear Father, I find myself doing things out of fear or to cope with the pain I'm experiencing. Please help me to discern what's truly helping me and my children stay safe, and what things I may need to gently course correct. I long to grow into the woman You created me to be—not the one that is just merely surviving. Amen.

Reflection:

Reflect on any habits or coping mechanisms you may have developed because of the challenges in your marriage—over or under eating, over-punishing your children to prevent your husband from harshly disciplining them, people pleasing, or withdrawing. Notice these things without judgment and consider if they're keeping you safe, or if you need to make some adjustments to keep growing and healing.

Pause. Take a deep breath. What's one small step in your healing you can celebrate today?

Speaking Your Story Safely

Building Strength Phase

This is the season where you begin to find your voice. Be prepared, it can feel messy at times to know when and how to use it. It's much like the struggle the butterfly goes through after its long, silent transformation in the cocoon. As if obeying some unknown signal, it finally bursts free—but not before this one last crucial phase.

From the outside, the butterfly's struggle in the cocoon looks like a near defeat. It fights, wrestles, and wriggles. This takes time and can appear painful, even futile—but oh, what we don't see! As the butterfly wrestles, that very motion is what pumps fluid down into its wings that it needs to fly. God uses its struggle to give it strength. I know it's hard to believe when you feel bedraggled and exhausted, but God can use your struggles to make you stronger, too.

Consider your voice in the same way. After living in an unsafe or unsustainable marriage, your voice may have been silenced or confused. Just like the butterfly strengthens its wings by pressing the bounds of its chrysalis, you too, will need to press the boundaries of what once held you captive, as you learn to share your truth safely and authentically.

In this section, you'll discover how to share your story wisely—with God first, then with safe people who will honor your heart. You'll learn to recognize safe voices from others, how to avoid those that shame, and how to speak your truth in love while staying grounded in who God created you to be. This phase may stretch you or feel uncomfortable at times, but don't shy away; this is the very season that God can use to strengthen you for true freedom.

Day 55
Rebuilding Identity in Christ

"They will rebuild the ancient ruins and restore the places long devastated; they will renew the ruined cities that have been devastated for generations."

Isaiah 61:4

———Pause. Take a few deep breaths. Now rest—and abide in Him.———

One thing that trauma, abuse, betrayal, and addiction all have in common for those on the receiving end is this—they try to steal our sense of identity.

They come into our lives like a bomb, sending shrapnel into the deepest recesses of our soul.

The betrayal whispers, "You're not good enough."

Abuse shouts, "You don't matter."

And pornography screams, "You'll never be as wanted or beautiful as the images on the screen."

Living with someone whose destructive behavior is fueled by alcohol, drugs, pornography, or narcissism can leave you feeling isolated, confused, and hopeless.

This is where we begin to prayerfully wage war against the lies that trauma has tried to write on our hearts. Rebuilding your identity as a daughter of the King takes time and intention. It's letting God step into the rubble and replace the shrapnel with His truth.

No, you may not return to the person you were before the bomb went off. But maybe that's not the goal.

When I was trained how to counsel crisis victims, the first step was to consider safety. In the aftermath of a natural disaster, we aren't helping them work on future plans. The goal is to stabilize the ground under their feet. We need to ensure they have the basics in place: shelter, food, warmth, reassurance. This is not an easy time; shock and overwhelm can freeze a person emotionally. They're just surviving at this point.

That's what trauma recovery looks like also. Begin by finding safety—emotionally, spiritually, and physically. You rest. You breathe. You let your soul know it's safe.

Once the dust begins to settle, that's when the rebuilding begins. You start to assess the damage—what was lost, what still stands, what can be salvaged. You slowly rediscover your footing—your sense of community, belonging, and voice.

Yes, you have lost much. But you have also survived much. And now you are here, in the rebuilding stage.

When someone loses everything in a disaster, it's natural to want to recreate what once was. But that version of life is gone. Instead, survivors begin to rebuild what fits the new landscape—a landscape that holds both the pain and the possibility.

You can rebuild on a new landscape, too. You may not return to life as it once was—but you can build something stronger.

Rebuilding your identity isn't so much about recovery as it is about resurrection. The "new you" isn't the woman you used to be. You're becoming stronger and wiser—more grounded in the truth. So, as you rebuild, don't lay your new foundation with old patterns—people-pleasing or performance—but from a place of peace.

Lean into your values, your principles, and your beliefs. These will be the core from which you make your future decisions, no longer based on desperation or what others want for you, but on what God has already placed inside you.

You're not starting at ground zero—this time you're starting from the truth. Remember, you're not behind—you're becoming.

Prayer:

Dear Father, thank You for being with me and helping me find safety in the aftermath of my disaster. Now, please help me to rebuild, and help me create a life that is stronger, richer, and more fulfilling than before. Amen.

Reflection:

Identify what was lost: What qualities, beliefs, or passions that you held before the trauma, abuse, or betrayal were dismissed or stolen from you? Name them.

Name what remains: What values, strengths, or truths do you hold today? List them. How can you honor these in the life you're rebuilding? Even small acts, words, habits, or choices can affirm these.

Declare your identity: Write a note to yourself from God's perspective—I have one myself; I call it my "Dear Darah" letter. Write down the truths you hear Him saying about you: "I am capable," or "I am a daughter of the King," "I am loveable," "I am brave." Then place it somewhere you can see it often, as a daily reminder of who *God* says you are.

—Pause. Take a deep breath. What's one small step in your healing you can celebrate today?

Day 56

Rewriting the Story of Shame

"By faith the prostitute Rahab, because she welcomed the spies, was not killed with those who were disobedient."

Hebrews 11:31

——*Pause. Take a few deep breaths. Now rest—and abide in Him.*——

Let me share a story with you. It's a story you may already know... but maybe you haven't looked at it quite this way.

It's the story of Rahab in the Bible. It's the story of prostitution—and it's a story of shame and a woman who was marginalized and probably felt forgotten by God—at first, anyway.

In Rahab's world, people looked down on prostitutes. In today's world it hasn't changed.

In Rahab's world, I imagine she must have felt desperate, or she wouldn't have given her body for money. Desperation drives us to do many things we wouldn't otherwise do, which can lead to feelings of shame.

I think about Rahab and imagine the deep shame she may have carried because of her occupation, enduring sneers and condescending glares wherever she went. She likely felt unworthy, overlooked, and "less than" in the eyes of those around her.

But then one day, she learns about some spies coming into her land. She had heard of these people... and more importantly about their God. And she believes their God is big and capable. Capable of destroying her people and her entire land. So, she makes a bold choice. She places herself in harm's way to protect God's spies—His entire nation, in fact.

Suddenly, her story shifts. Rahab the prostitute steps into the limelight of history—not defined by her "profession" or the deception she used to protect God's spies. No, God finishes writing her story a different way. Her one decision to do something different—to follow God—changes her entire life and the lives of generations to come.

Rahab is no longer the prostitute, but rather the hero.

Rahab is no longer the lonely woman, but the woman who marries into the nation of Israel.

Rahab is no longer destitute and destined to give her body for money but rather becomes esteemed and part of the lineage of royalty to come. Rahab, in fact, becomes the mother of Boaz, which places her in the line of King David and eventually Christ Himself. Through Rahab comes the Savior of the world.

Rahab didn't stay stuck in shame because of what she used to do. She didn't let the snickers, the glares, the words of others, or the heavy cloak of shame she might have felt hold her back. She chose to do a bold thing despite her past—and God gave her a new future.

I know what shame feels like, and maybe you do, too. Shame speaks deep inside our hearts and tells us we are bad or broken. But I love how Rahab's life so clearly shows how a person can break free from those rusty chains of shame. And I love that God is showing us that we can change the course of our story, too.

Your story may feel completely different than Rahab's, but shame is universal. And often, after abuse, separation, divorce, or being in a relationship where you've been demeaned and mistreated or even told you were of little value, shame rears its nasty head. But God is inviting you to rewrite your story.

You don't have to stay stuck in the loop of shame or what others think about you. Rahab had to take a bold step of faith for her story to change. You, too, may need to take a bold step.

Your story can end differently than your story began, because God is in the business of rewriting stories for His glory.

Prayer:

Dear Father, thank You for the story of Rahab. Though her story may be different from mine, I feel that same sense of shame. Help me hold my head high and take the bold steps You're calling me to take. I long to leave shame behind and embrace a life where I can truly thrive.

Reflection:

What situations or experiences have stirred feelings of shame in you, and what does God's truth say about who you really are?

–Pause. Take a deep breath. What's one small step in your healing you– can celebrate today?

Day 57
Reclaiming Home: Finding Peace Again

"Have not I commanded thee? Be strong and of a good courage; be not afraid, neither be thou dismayed: for the Lord thy God is with thee whithersoever thou goest."

Joshua 1:9, KJV

———*Pause. Take a few deep breaths. Now rest—and abide in Him.*———

Leaving Papua New Guinea, where we'd been living as missionaries, was as traumatic as our arrival. I had gotten over my initial culture shock, grown to adore our new home, and fallen in love with the people and places. And then, suddenly, it all fell apart.

One day, my husband told me he no longer wanted to stay. We'd sold almost everything we owned, spent months reassuring our family we'd be safe, and the mission had invested time and resources in us. Then there was someone far more precious — John Phillip, the baby we had named, held, and loved, and were in the process of adopting. So many prayers were being answered in Papua New Guinea—full-time mission service and finally expanding our family. Our son had been praying so earnestly and *specifically* for a baby *brother*.

John Phillip, the people, the country—they had *all* become home to me.

Then everything shifted. I won't go into the details, but I was devastated. Even as I'm writing this now, tears still well up when I think back.

We had no idea where we were going next, no money, and no assurance from the government that John Phillip could come with us. Then one day, standing at my bedroom window crying, I looked up and saw a bird sitting on a limb just outside my window.

Something in me latched on to that bird, and the ache of my heart flooded out in prayer. "God *if* You are truly with me, and You won't leave me, no matter where we go, then *prove it*. Make that bird stay there until I get home this evening." I finally picked myself up and took my son to the local Steak Haus pool to say goodbye to his friends as I had promised.

When we returned that evening, the bird was still there, and the next day when I woke to cry my heart out again, the bird was still on the limb. And for the next seven days, in the exact spot, every time I went to my window, there sat the bird. Dear friend, I've seen some amazing miracles in our time as missionaries—but none like that.

During that season of grief, God brought a verse to my heart: "Have not I commanded thee? Be strong and of a good courage; be not afraid, neither be thou dismayed: for the Lord thy God is with thee *whithersoever* thou goest." (Joshua 1:9, KJV). Something about that word—*whithersoever*—has stuck with me ever since.

At the week's end, our neighbor, an avid bird watcher, mentioned to me that we had a sacred kingfisher in our yard and how amazed he was that it had stayed there seven days, because they're normally reclusive birds. More confirmation to my weary heart—God *would* be with us wherever we called home.

Since then, home for my son and I has shifted more times than we can count. But one thing I've learned is that home becomes what we make of it. Every move we've made, I've kept one photo close (and now a painting from my son): that little bird on a limb. It reminds me that wherever God places us, He is with us—because He promised He would be.

John Phillip never officially became a part of our family, because God had other plans for his home as well. His mother, who had originally wanted to end her pregnancy, but agreed to allow us to adopt him, had a change of heart after we left and chose to raise him. We stepped into his life just long enough to protect him before birth and to give him a safe home with the mother God had already chosen for him.

Sweet friend, you may be facing leaving your home, starting over, or even staying put—but it's not the same as it once was. Safety may not look like what you used to call home. Yet the same God, who kept that bird on a limb and protected John Phillip, on the other side of the world, is the God who sees you now and will be with you, *whithersoever* you go.

Prayer:

Dear Heavenly Father, my home has changed, my heart aches for things to be the way they once were. Hold me close in Your arms when I feel displaced and uncertain and be my dwelling place and my peace, here or whithersoever I go. Amen.

Reflection:

Leaving things behind is painful. Take time to allow space for grieving—maybe it's your pets, your home, your church family, or the life you once knew.

Reflect on the following: What does "home" mean to you now? How has that meaning changed? In what ways have you begun to experience peace and safety in your current space, even if it's small or temporary?

If home doesn't yet feel peaceful, what's one small step you can take to nurture your peace—maybe creating a reset space, where your nervous system can rest, a quiet corner with a comfy chair and a cozy blanket? Remember, even a small, imperfect space can become a spot to retreat to when you need peace.

–Pause. Take a deep breath. What's one small step in your healing you can celebrate today?

Day 58
Challenging Your Inner Critic

"Behold what manner of love the Father has bestowed on us, that we should be called children of God!"
1 John 3:1, NKJV

———*Pause. Take a few deep breaths. Now rest—and abide in Him.*———

When I was little, we used to chant, "Sticks and stones may break my bones, but words will never hurt me!" I was a pretty exuberant kiddo, so I probably added a cheeky "na-na, na-na, boo-boo" at the end!

But as I grew into my teen years, I quickly learned that words *do* hurt—and often leave marks deeper than any bruise ever could.

In junior high and high school, I was bullied mercilessly. I learned to hide and harden my heart so I could avoid being hurt. But my deep desire to be loved, while not yet knowing my worth, left me vulnerable. I experienced things I never should have—sexual abuse as a teen, a pregnancy at seventeen that ended in miscarriage, years of navigating a spouse's addictions, betrayal, emotional abuse, and threats of physical harm.

Even writing this now, I can feel the weight of it all. And yet, by God's grace, I truly am a survivor.

Those early wounds didn't break me—but for a while they shaped my inner critic. For years, it whispered, "I'm not good enough. Why bother trying—I'll probably just fail. No one could ever really love me."

Maybe you've heard similar lies—from childhood, from school, or in your marriage. Maybe you've been gaslit, told your feelings don't matter, or made to believe your needs were unreasonable.

Perhaps as a child you were labeled "too much," "too sensitive," or made to feel small. And so now you minimize yourself as others have done to you. But here's the truth: Putting ourselves down is not humility—it's devaluing God's handiwork. Speaking kindly about and to ourselves isn't prideful or selfish (*as some would have us believe*), it's honoring the One who created us. Because God *never* makes things of low worth. And you, dear friend, are no exception.

When we learn to view ourselves the way God does, we begin to see the gifts and strengths He already placed within us. We start to believe that we can accomplish more than we ever imagined—because we're no longer doing it alone. His power is made perfect in our weakness (2 Corinthians 12:9). That means even in the places that feel broken, His strength shines the brightest.

When we compare ourselves to others, obsess over our failures, or beat ourselves up for honest mistakes, we create a mental loop that says, "I can't." But, with God, we absolutely can. His strength equips us to rise above the lies and limitations others have imposed.

If you struggle believing your worth after trauma or abuse, start small by allowing God to replace those old messages with His truth. Let Him remind you that you are seen, chosen, and deeply loved (Jeremiah 1:5, Jeremiah 31:3).

You are not too sensitive. You are not too much (and really—who gets to decide that anyway!)

You, my friend, are a beloved daughter of the Most High King.

Prayer:

Dear Heavenly Father, I sometimes get stuck repeating the lies others have told me about myself. Help me to replace them with Your truth and to remember who I truly am in Your eyes. Amen.

Reflection:

Think about some of the things others have said to you or ways they've made you feel. What lies have you internalized about yourself, and how could you begin to reframe those with truth?

–Pause. Take a deep breath. What's one small step in your healing you can celebrate today?

Day 59
God Believes You, Even if Others Don't

"But they did not believe the women, because their words seemed to them like nonsense."
Luke 24:11

——*Pause. Take a few deep breaths. Now rest—and abide in Him.*——

It was a group of women who discovered the body of Jesus was gone—the tomb was empty. They rushed to tell the news to the apostles. "But they did not believe the women, because their words seemed to them like nonsense" (Luke 24:11).

Like these women, you may have tried to reach out to those at your church or even your family to seek support—but were dismissed or treated as though your words "seemed like nonsense" to them. If so, I see you. More importantly, God sees you.

God believes the stories of women, even if others don't. In fact, He often used them to be truth tellers. God used the woman at the well to tell others of Him despite her history of shame. He used Tamar, who men tried to silence, to speak the truth.

Jesus was also deeply invested in the healing of women. The woman with the flow of blood had been dismissed and avoided for years. While others turned away from her, Jesus turned toward her and healed her, saying, "Daughter, thy faith hath made thee whole; go in peace, and be whole of thy plague" (Mark 5:34, KJV).

Maybe you've tried to share what's happening in your marriage, but you weren't believed. Maybe you were sent right back into the chaos and dysfunction, armed with "marriage tips" but no real support. If so, please know God believes you.

He has shown His heart again and again, in Scripture, toward women as they struggle against injustice and pain. While Hannah was at the temple crying her heart out to God because of the deep mistreatment in her home, the officiating priest, instead of consoling her, turned and *accused her* of being drunk. Yet God saw her weeping, answered her prayers, gave her a child and, in due time, anointed *him* priest.

Sadly, it is not an uncommon story for women to finally summon the strength to seek help and support, only to be told they're imagining things or to have their situation dismissed—or worse, to be told, "I need to hear the other side of the story."

Sweet friend, in cases of betrayal, abuse, and addiction, there aren't two sides writing the story anymore. There is one painful story—and it's that your life is being destroyed, either slowly and silently or abruptly and violently.

If you go to someone to bravely share your story and they don't believe you or dismiss you, heed the words of Jesus: "If anyone will not welcome you or listen to your words, leave that home or town and shake the dust off your feet" (Matthew 10:14). Not being believed can cause secondary trauma, so don't stay long where others have proven they aren't to be trusted with your story.

This is too important to let others silence you. God doesn't silence you. He hears you, sees you, and believes you. And He is also ready to heal you—because He cares that deeply for you.

Prayer:

Dear Father, I've held my story silent for too long, and I desire healing. Guide me to the support I need and help me share what needs to be shared. Lead me to safe people and spaces where my story can be brought into the light without shame or doubt. Amen.

Reflection:

Creating an authentic, safe support system is vital for healing. If you haven't found this yet, where could you begin to look—an abuse-informed counselor, a trusted friend, a support group? And if you already have support, are there ways you can deepen those connections?

—Pause. Take a deep breath. What's one small step in your healing you can celebrate today?

Day 60
Sharing Your Story on Holy Ground

"I pour out my complaint before Him;
I declare before Him my trouble."

Psalm 142:2

——*Pause. Take a few deep breaths. Now rest—and abide in Him.*——

Do you need a secret place where just you and God can meet because it feels like you have nowhere else for your story to land? Maybe others have denied, dismissed, minimized what you've been through—or perhaps you fear that others have grown weary of hearing your story. Yet you still have more to process. We all need a place to be real and raw before God—and with ourselves.

You are not alone. God's people have long experienced heartache and sorrow. The Psalms are the overflow of such pain. David took his pen and let the anguish of his heart flow out onto the pages we now read. You can, too. God wants to bring you clarity amid your pain, just as He did for the psalmist, who said, "When I tried to understand all this, it troubled me deeply till I entered the sanctuary of God; then I understood" (Psalm 73:16-17).

You, too, can create a sanctuary space right where you are. Remember when Moses met with God at the burning bush? God said "This is holy ground" (Exodus 3:5). The bush wasn't holy or inherently special—it was holy because God's presence was there.

Many women have found solace in expressing themselves through the pages of a journal and pouring out their pain to God. When you invite His presence to be with you as you write, those pages become your holy ground—a sacred place to hold the things that feel too heavy to carry on your own. It doesn't have to be fancy. It could even be the notes app on your phone—just somewhere you can offload the deepest aches that keep you awake at night.

But maybe your heart feels too heavy even for words on a page. If so, then let your prayers become the ink. Let the overflow of your heart rise to Him in prayer. Let Him meet you in your prayer closet, on a quiet walk, or wherever you are. Remember, it's His presence that makes it sacred, not your effort or location.

Sweet friend, we all need a place to release our story and our pain. Wherever you meet with God in truth, *that* is holy ground. Let Him hold you and your story in that sacred place today.

Prayer:

Dear God, please help me to release the pain I've been holding on to. Give me an outlet where I can express myself and know that I am safe. Amen.

Reflection:

Would it feel safe to write your story to God—between just you and Him? Set aside a few quiet moments to journal what's been happening, how you feel, and where you long for His help. Let it also be a place to record the good moments in the midst of the hard, so your heart can hold the good and release the bad.

Writing can be both a sacred way to pour out your heart—and a wise way to keep a clear record of events happening in your marriage should you need them later on.

–Pause. Take a deep breath. What's one small step in your healing you can celebrate today?

Day 61
Choosing the Good Despite the Hard

"I praise you because I am fearfully and wonderfully made; your works are wonderful, I know that full well."
Psalm 139:14

——*Pause. Take a few deep breaths. Now rest—and abide in Him.*——

One morning while I was out walking, something unexpected happened. At the time, my son and I were living in a camper, parked in a church member's field. I was newly separated and facing a season so heavy it felt like it was swallowing me whole. Everything felt unstable and uncertain.

We had just moved back from South America, where we lived and served as missionaries. Our hearts were still there, not in that field. We had returned to the U.S. with only enough money to purchase a used vehicle that my husband would use for work.

We had no real place to call home, no extra money, and no idea what life would look like next. Normally, transition didn't shake me. We had lived in various mission fields relying on God to sustain us—and He always had. But, this time was different. The stress was seeping into every corner of my heart, and something inside of me began to crack. I didn't want to admit it, but bitterness was settling in. My patience had worn thin and my spirit felt tired and worn.

And that's exactly where God met me. As I walked that morning, I poured out everything—my bitterness, my discontent, my fears, my challenges, and especially my anger. Where I was agitated, He was still. Where I was restless, He was steady. Where I had a complaining spirit, His patience began to soften me.

Somewhere along that gravel road, as I cried out to God, giving Him my every ache, He began to subdue the rage and hurt swelling in my heart. I felt myself become still before Him. And then a phrase came into my mind. Quiet at first—then again, stronger: "Instead of complaint, choose the good."

It stopped me. It felt like both a correction and a comfort.

As I continued walking, God gently pulled my mind away from my problems and toward Him. I began to notice the tiny wildflowers growing along the road that I hadn't noticed before, and as I did, the phrase came again: "Instead of complaint, choose the good." So I did. I thanked God for the flowers.

A few steps later, I noticed the trees swaying in the wind, and the blue sky I had been walking under all along. It was everything I had been too consumed to see. And again: "Choose the good." So I did. One small praise at a time.

It continued on this way until I felt broken before God. I was so tired of the bitterness that had taken root in my heart, tired of my discontent and woundedness…simply tired. It was then that I surrendered. Even though I had been a Christian for years, it became clear just how much baggage I had been dragging behind me. That day, I decided to place it all into the hands of the One who could actually carry it.

I gave Him my hurt, my wounds, my anger, and my need to control my circumstances. And in exchange, I chose, however imperfectly, to "choose the good" in front of me.

As I walked, I felt the shift. In my mind I kept repeating the phrase "choose the good." Before long, I was saying it out loud almost as if I was challenging myself; I would no longer live hindered by my bitterness and discouragement! I would "choose the good!" I can still remember the peace that washed over me. It was like a balm over my long-neglected wounds.

And here's what I've come to understand since that morning: choosing the good isn't about ignoring the bad. It isn't pretending everything is fine. It's getting into alignment with how God designed our minds and hearts to heal. Long before research told us that gratitude rewires our brains, lowers stress, and restores peace, God had already spoken: "Do not be anxious about anything, but in every situation, by prayer and petition, with thanksgiving, present your requests to God. And the peace of God, which transcends all understanding, will guard your hearts and your minds (Philippians 4:6-7).[1,2]

God invites us to thankfulness not because He needs it—but because *we* do. Gratitude isn't a dismissal of our pain; it's a pathway to healing. It turns our eyes toward the God who restores, strengthens, and steadies us when life feels impossible.

So if you're reading this and your heart feels heavy, start small. One good thing. Nothing is too little. God doesn't need our grand gestures or perfect words—He is ready to meet us in our mess and wants to help us heal right where we are.

Prayer:

Dear Father, help me to keep a soft heart that remembers the blessings You've given me even when this life feels hard. Thank you, Lord, for Your Word that tells me I don't have to continue to be harmed, and that You want good things for me and my children— help us to move toward the good and away from the bad. Amen.

Reflection:

Take a moment and thank God for the good things you have and are experiencing, even amid the hard times.

–Pause. Take a deep breath. What's one small step in your healing you can celebrate today?

Day 62
Speaking Up Like Abigail

"I meant that you are not to associate with anyone who claims to be a believer yet indulges in sexual sin, or is greedy, or worships idols, or is abusive, or is a drunkard, or cheats people. Don't even eat with such people."
1 Corinthians 5:11, NLT

———Pause. Take a few deep breaths. Now rest—and abide in Him.———

In many Christian spaces, biblical marriage is described as a husband being the head of the home and a wife being his helpmeet. But what happens when "helping" doesn't look like submission, but rather courageous truth-telling? What if being a godly wife also means standing up to ungodly behavior and protecting God's image in your home?

The story of Abigail in the Bible gives us a beautiful picture of this. It's a picture of wisdom and bravery in the face of abuse. If you haven't read it, I would highly encourage you to (1 Samuel 25). Abigail was married to a foolish "scoundrel" named Nabal. He was arrogant, entitled, lacked empathy, and selfish—he had all the markers of what today we would call narcissism.

Because of her husband, Abigail was put into a very hard situation. Maybe because of your husband's nature, you've been put in hard situations before, too. Nabal's arrogance nearly led to his whole family's destruction. So, Abigail acted swiftly—not in rebellion, but in righteousness. She went against her husband's wishes, took initiative, and prevented bloodshed.

In doing so, she shows us that being a "helpmeet" isn't about blind obedience and submission. It's about helping in a way that honors God, even when it means confronting your husband's wrongdoing.

Too often women in unsafe or unsustainable marriages are told that submission means silence, and that silence is godliness. But Scripture tells a different story. The Bible speaks very clearly about those who harm, deceive, or exploit and abuse others—this includes an abusive or adulterous spouse. Scripture warns us to not partner with that kind of darkness. So, lean in close, dear friend, as God speaks to you through His word.

"I meant that you are not to associate with anyone who claims to be a believer yet indulges in sexual sin, or is greedy, or worships idols, or is abusive, or is a drunkard, or cheats people. Don't even eat with such people" (1 Corinthians 5:11, NLT).

"But if anyone does not provide for his own, and especially for those of his household, he has denied the faith and is worse than an unbeliever" (1 Timothy 5:8, NKJV).

"But mark this: There will be terrible times in the last days. People will be lovers of themselves, lovers of money, boastful, proud, abusive, disobedient to their parents, ungrateful, unholy, without love, unforgiving, slanderous, without self-control, brutal, not lovers of the good, treacherous, rash, conceited, lovers of pleasure rather than lovers of God—having a form of godliness but denying its power. Have nothing to do with such people" (2 Timothy 3:1-5).

"Reject a divisive man after the first and second admonition, knowing that such a person is warped and sinning, being self-condemned" (Titus 3:10-11, NKJV).

"How can you make a partnership out of right and wrong? That's not partnership; that's war. Is light best friends with dark? Does Christ go strolling with the Devil? Do trust and mistrust hold hands?" (2 Corinthians 6:14-16, MSG).

Dear friend, God does not call you to protect sin. He calls you to protect your heart and soul—and I will go so far as to say, your husband's as well. Because if he is behaving like Nabal, sometimes the only thing that can awaken him to *his* sin and save his soul is strong, God-honoring boundaries—or, if needed, putting distance between yourself and his destructive choices.

Abigail's story reminds us that speaking truth is not rebellion— it's righteousness. It takes courage to confront evil, and even more to walk away from it. Remember, you are not alone—the same God who was guiding Abigail is here to guide you, too.

Prayer:

Dear Father, please help me to be a brave and wise helpmeet—one who loves truth more than approval and who does not stay silent in the face of wrong. Give me the courage to take a stand when it's needed, wisdom to know when to act, and protection as I walk in obedience to You. Amen.

Reflection:

Is God asking you to show bravery like Abigail, and if so, what does that look like? Are there situations where you've hesitated to speak truth or set a boundary because you feared it would go against God's will? In light of Abigail's story, how do you see those things now?

–Pause. Take a deep breath. What's one small step in your healing you– can celebrate today?

Day 63
Reclaiming Your Authentic Voice

*"It is of the Lord's mercies that we are not consumed,
because his compassions fail not."*
Lamentations 3:22, KJV

———*Pause. Take a few deep breaths. Now rest—and abide in Him.*———

While out walking one morning, I passed a friend along the way and asked how she was doing. Her response was one I had given many times myself, especially to those not in my "closest" circle: "Well, I can't complain—God is good."

Then she asked, "How about you?" Normally—no, almost always—I'd respond, "I can't complain, either. God has been good to me, too!" *But not this day.* Instead, something far more truthful slipped out before I could filter it: "Well, truthfully, I can complain—I've gotten quite good at it, in fact… but I know I shouldn't!"

We both laughed, but inside, I felt the deep truth of my words. That week had been hard. I didn't have the energy to say what wasn't true. And really, why should I? I needed to be authentic.

My marriage was falling apart, and I didn't want to hide behind polite small talk that didn't match my heart.

Many of us have learned to hide our feelings and mask our struggles—especially if we've lived with criticism, control, or abuse, which taught us to silence our feelings. We learned it was safer to smile and say, "I'm fine," even if we're breaking on the inside.

When your voice has been silenced, questioned, or dismissed for so long, speaking the truth can feel risky—but it's where healing begins.

Perfection and authenticity rarely walk hand in hand. Because authenticity means truth. And Scripture tells us not one of us is perfect aside from Christ. God calls us to live in truth, not pretense. Sometimes life is messy, dark, and hard. But even there, "It is of the Lord's mercies that we are not consumed, because His compassions fail not" (Lamentation 3:22).

Sweet sister, it's OK to take off the mask and be real. It's OK to have down days and feel weary—you've been through a lot. God meets you right where you are and whispers, "You don't have to pretend with Me."

Prayer:

Dear Father, I'm tired, weary, and don't have the energy to keep up appearances any longer. Help me to be real and authentic before You and others. I need to be able to share my heart in order to truly heal. Give me wisdom and discernment to know when and with whom it is safe to share the deeper parts of my heart. Thank You for meeting me right where I am and loving me in my honesty. Amen.

Reflection:

What masks are you tempted to wear, and what would it look like to lay them down before God and with safe others in your life? How can you hold space for both gratitude and honesty—choosing thankfulness as Scripture calls us to, while still being real when the pain cuts deep?

—Pause. Take a deep breath. What's one small step in your healing you can celebrate today?

Day 64
Learning to Say: "This is What Really Happened"

"For though the righteous fall seven times, they rise again, but the wicked stumble when calamity strikes."
Proverbs 24:16

——*Pause. Take a few deep breaths. Now rest—and abide in Him.*——

I've worked with many survivors who struggle to clearly say what happened in their marriage, or who told me that what happened to them was their fault. They don't always come out and say it that directly, but it's there: "I allowed this to happen because I didn't leave." Or, " I knew he was like this, *before* we married."

Friend, let's start there today. Because maybe you, too, have had these thoughts.

Saying the harm was your fault because you stayed is like saying it's your fault for getting into a car and being hit by someone else.

I was once in a car accident with my son where we were hit by a drunk driver. I didn't do anything wrong. I got in the car and trusted that the other drivers on the road were going to be responsible. That's what most of us do. It's the same in relationships; we trust that others will follow the rules, act decently, and not put us in danger.

When someone chooses to be reckless or to cause harm, that's their fault—not ours.

But I hear you, maybe you did notice your husband had some problems before you got married—a temper, a controlling streak, a bit too much drinking—but you had no way to know how far that would go. I'm sure you hoped he would make better choices.

Blaming yourself because you saw hints would be like me saying, "I saw the driver's car parked outside a bar earlier that night; I *should* have known he'd get drunk later on, cross the centerline, total my vehicle, and almost kill my son and me—it's *all* my fault."

Trusting someone, especially someone who is supposed to love you, isn't a flaw and it doesn't make you foolish. It's what emotionally healthy people do. The fault for the harm lies with the person who betrayed the trust or refused to get healthy. We can't take responsibility for someone else's dysfunction. Yet we often do.

When that person gaslights you, manipulates you, or when others join in and victim-blame you, the confusion and self-doubt can deepen. It becomes even harder to trust your own voice, to believe your version of what happened. But friend, that's why reclaiming your voice matters so much in this process of healing.

Often when we stay in relationships with someone who is abusive, deceptive, narcissistic—you name what "it" is—we do so because we're compassionate, empathetic people. We love the person, or we wouldn't have chosen to marry them. We're simply treating them with the same respect and dignity we would give anyone. The difference is that an emotionally healthy person would reciprocate that love and care, while a harmful person just takes advantage of it.

You weren't wrong for having a heart that reflects Christ. What's wrong is that your husband doesn't. It's OK, beloved, to say, "My husband hurt me." "My husband abused me." "My husband cheated on me." Whatever *it* was, it's OK—and healthy—to be able to say: "This is what happened." And it's OK to create space now if you're not safe. You get to speak your story without the enemy's lies clouding it.

Learning to speak what happened isn't about blaming or staying stuck in the past; it's about clearly naming the truth. Because each time you do, the fog of confusion lifts a little more, and your voice grows stronger.

Prayer:

Dear God, there were times when I may have seen things in my husband but wasn't ready to fully acknowledge them yet. Help me to extend grace to myself, and to understand that my empathy is not a weakness—even if it's been taken advantage of. Help me to speak my truth now without blaming myself. Amen.

Reflection:

What truth do you need to speak to yourself today? And how can you release any self-blame for what you may have noticed and focus instead on what steps you can take now?

–Pause. Take a deep breath. What's one small step in your healing you can celebrate today?

Day 65
Speaking the Truth in Love

"'No,' they replied, 'there may not be enough for both us and you. Instead, go to those who sell oil and buy some for yourselves.'"

Matthew 25:9

——*Pause. Take a few deep breaths. Now rest—and abide in Him.*——

Did you know there is a difference in the Bible between being kind and being nice? There's a story in the Bible that author Leslie Vernick uses to illustrate the difference, and I think it's quite powerful.

In the Bible, we're told of ten virgins all attending a wedding feast. Five of them in the story are called wise, and five are called foolish. The five that God calls wise had been storing up their oil for a future time; they had been planning and preparing. The five that God calls foolish had not. And here's where the story gets *very* interesting. The foolish virgins notice the oil to light their lamps has gone out. So, they go to the five wise virgins and ask them to share some of their oil. Now pause.

Dear friend, lean in closely as I share this next part, because I don't want you to miss it.

The wise virgins replied, "No, there may not be enough for both us and you. Instead, go to those who sell oil and buy some for yourselves" (Matthew 25:9-11). Now stop.

Could you even imagine saying no to someone asking such a seemingly simple request—we would be aghast! That's not what *nice* girls are supposed to do, right? We're always supposed to be nice and accommodating, *right*?

Maybe you weren't taught this, but growing up in the deep South, where pleasantries take precedence over authenticity, I sure was.

Now, back to the story: The results of that no were that the five foolish virgins went away to look for oil and missed out on the wedding feast. And yet, as God penned this story, He commended the five wise virgins for their firm response and boundary.

In today's society, it might not have sounded nice, but God knew it was important that they speak their truth.

If they had given a part of their oil away, neither they nor the five foolish virgins would have had enough to make it through the night, as the feast lingered into the wee hours of the morning. They were called wise for protecting their resources, and they did so firmly, but kindly. If they hadn't, they too, would have missed the wedding feast.

Beloved, in this story the wedding feast is an analogy for God's second coming and spending eternity with our groom, Jesus. Had they not been firm, and instead, given the little resources they had, they wouldn't have been able to be with Jesus.

The same is true for us. We only have so many resources—time, energy, focus, finances. We're called to be wise with what we have also. And if we allow others who behave foolishly to use up our limited resources with their foolishness, we may miss out on spending time with God too. We're even told that by walking with a foolish person we can begin to take on their ways. God doesn't want that for us.

Friend, the word *nice* is nowhere in the Bible, only the word *kind*. God calls us to speak our truth in kindness. We can set boundaries and speak up for ourselves kindly, yet firmly, and when we do so, God calls us wise, too.

Prayer:

Dear Father, please teach me how to let my "yes" be yes, and my "no" be no. Teach me to set boundaries with kindness and firmness, without carrying guilt—especially with those who try to drain my time and energy with their foolishness. Amen.

Reflection:

Who in your life do you need to be firmer with, or set a boundary around, and what might that look like? Remember some boundaries are non-negotiable while others are preferential—you get to decide which is which and what the consequences will be if they're crossed.

–Pause. Take a deep breath. What's one small step in your healing you can celebrate today?

Day 66
How Much to Share and When

"One who has unreliable friends soon comes to ruin, but there is a friend who sticks closer than a brother."
Proverbs 18:24

———*Pause. Take a few deep breaths. Now rest—and abide in Him.*———

Have you ever experienced a vulnerability hangover? Where you shared a part of your story or life with someone and then left the conversation feeling a deep churning discomfort and shame for having shared something so personal? I have. And it isn't pretty!

Suddenly we feel exposed and vulnerable, fearing the other person will judge or reject us. We may even fear that person will share our private story with others. It's already emotionally exhausting to dredge up the most intimate bits of our life. Being vulnerable can even trigger physiological reactions—our heart beats faster, our palms sweat, or we feel nauseous while sharing—or after as we replay the experience. We're left reeling or questioning why we ever shared in the first place!

After this, those overwhelming feelings of the "hangover" can cause us to withdraw, ruminate on the conversation, or swear to ourselves we'll never do that again!

Dear friend, if this is you, give yourself grace. Allow yourself time after the experience to recover gently. Don't beat yourself up—most of us have been there at one time or another. And those of us with trauma, probably more than others.

While we need to listen in part to these feelings, in part we need to challenge them. Sometimes these feelings can indicate that we've shared with someone who isn't safe to hold our story because their response makes that clear.

Scripture warns us of this when it says, "Don't cast your pearls before swine" (Matthew 7:6, NKJV). We don't have to give what's precious to those who won't treat it that way. While other times, being authentic and vulnerable may simply be unfamiliar—and that can feel scary.

Maybe you were taught never to share your pain, or to "just suck it up," so you don't want to come across as needy. If this is the case, use these experiences to challenge yourself and grow. Practice healthy disclosure with safe people you can trust and start learning how to share your story—in layers. God gives us a principle in Ecclesiastes 3:7: There is a "time to keep silence, and a time to speak."

Some people will not be safe to hold your story. And some people may be safe to only hold parts of your story. In those instances, it's wise to stay silent or partially silent, because sharing too much could put you in an unsafe position. We'll talk more about that tomorrow.

But there are also safe people—seek those people and find solace and support in them. Don't allow anyone to use Scripture or other writings to convince you that you shouldn't speak up about the wrongs in your marriage. Speaking up is not you being disloyal to your vows—it's being a good steward of your mind, body, and children.

God wants us to share and be vulnerable with others. He has called us to "carry each other's burdens," and goes on to say that when this happens, it "fulfills the law of Christ" (Galatians 6:2). There are safe people out there who are able to shoulder your burdens—don't be afraid to let them in. You don't have to carry everything alone.

Prayer:

Dear Lord, help me to discern when it's safe and how much to reveal. And in those moments when I feel uneasy or I regret opening up—especially in a safe space—help me to extend grace and compassion to myself. Amen.

Reflection/Action Steps:

If you experience a vulnerability hangover, remember it's often your nervous system reacting. Treat yourself tenderly, take deep breaths, find a safe space, and name what you're feeling. Reflect on those emotions with compassion, practice relaxation techniques, and speak truth to your inner critic, replacing any lies with the truth about who you are.

Discomfort can feel unsettling, but it can also lead to growth and healing. You did a brave thing sharing a piece of your story— that vulnerability is actually strength. Don't let your body convince you otherwise.

Going forward it can help to keep your audience in mind. Test the waters to ensure they're safe and prepare what you want to say beforehand. If you're sharing with a safe person and still feel discomfort, breathe through it, remembering your body will take time to learn it's safe. Be patient with yourself!

–Pause. Take a deep breath. What's one small step in your healing you can celebrate today?

Day 67
When Sharing is Used Against You

"Discretion will protect you, and understanding will guard you."
Proverbs 2:11

——*Pause. Take a few deep breaths. Now rest—and abide in Him.*——

It's always healthy to have support when you're experiencing abuse, betrayal, or even the confusion that comes when mental illness or neurodivergence affects your marriage. Staying silent to protect your husband's image, because of shame or worry about being pitied, may feel safer, but it won't bring lasting healing. I remember what it felt like during our years serving in missions, while my marriage was quietly falling apart. I didn't know who I could trust to hold the weight of my painful truth.

Dear friend, stepping into this discomfort—though difficult—can be a path toward true freedom and healing.

However, it's also important to be wise in how you go about seeking that support. There are some very real things you need to be aware of, that I share, not to scare you from speaking up, but to help you share wisely and safely.

Sometimes, sharing with a mutual friend, a church member, or even a family member can lead to your story getting back to your husband, which may trigger retaliation or escalation. Even well-meaning people may try to confront him or simply not understand the danger of sharing.

This can also happen in counseling or in church settings. If you're sharing with a pastor, counselor, or mentor who isn't trauma- or abuse-informed, they might unintentionally pressure you to reconcile before it's safe. This aligns with what we discussed on day 16 about the dangers of couples counseling. In some churches, there may even be a culture of sharing private needs as public prayer requests—this can also put you at risk.

Social media is another place to be cautious. As you regain your voice and realize the injustice of your situation, it may be tempting to share parts of your story online—for comfort or to vent. But anything you share publicly, whether on social media, in emails, texts, or group messages, can be used as evidence.

As much as we may want to believe our spouse would never hurt us this way, I've seen it many times. An angry husband—or their attorney—may take statements out of context to make the survivor look vindictive, unstable, or untruthful. Your spouse may even claim you're trying to alienate your children and launch a "public campaign" to refute your story.

It's awful to have to protect yourself from the very one who promised to love and protect you in his vows, but I don't want you to be caught off guard; it happens. Yet Scripture reminds us, "Discretion *will* protect you, and understanding will guard you" (Proverbs 2:11, emphasis added).

If this is a part of your story, being wise is not the same as being deceptive; it's stewarding your heart and your children well.

And here's the hope that can sustain you, even in the midst of this pain: God is with you as you take each careful, wise step. You're not walking this path alone, and your courage, even in these discretions, is a witness to the life He is restoring in you. Let wisdom guide you sweet friend.

Prayer:

Dear God, thank You for guiding me wisely as I navigate this extremely hard situation. Help me protect myself and my children by being discerning about who I share our story with. At the same time, please surround me with support so I do not have to walk this journey alone. Amen.

Reflection:

Who are the safe people you've found to share your story with? If you haven't yet, who has shown discernment, trustworthiness, and compassion, who you might be able to reach out to for support?

–Pause. Take a deep breath. What's one small step in your healing you– can celebrate today?

Day 68
Building a Circle of Safety and a Tribe that Heals

"Two are better than one, because they have a good return for their labor: if either of them falls down, one can help the other up."

Ecclesiastes 4:9-10

——*Pause. Take a few deep breaths. Now rest—and abide in Him.*——

Jesus had what I call "circles of relationship." At the very center was His Father—His source, His anchor, His everything.

Next came His inner circle—the twelve disciples—those who walked closely with Him, sharing meals, ministry, and everyday life.

Beyond those were others who followed Him, believed in Him, and served alongside Him. Then came the crowds—those He ministered to with compassion but didn't invite into His private world.

And on the outer edge were those who opposed and rejected Him—people He still loved but wisely kept at a distance or away from completely at times.

Jesus loved *everyone*, in every circle, but He didn't grant everyone the same level of access to His life. He modeled healthy boundaries and healthy community. We need that, too.

If we modeled our relationships after Jesus's example, at the center would be our relationship with God. From there, our next circle would be our closest friends, the ones who get us even when we're bedraggled, messy, or two bad days away from talking to our houseplants!

Then comes the wider circle—those we care about and enjoy but don't share our deepest secrets with.

And finally, the outer circle—those we serve, encourage, and love as neighbors, but who may not be a part of our inner life.

When we understand our circles and our boundaries, we can love like Jesus did—freely, wisely, and without burning out. We protect our closest relationships and give space where it's needed in others, recognizing that as life changes, people may move in and out of our circles.

Building your tribe during this season of healing is vital. Take your time. Test the waters. Notice who has proven to be safe to invite closer and who might belong in a wider circle for now.

Years ago, I saw a documentary showing a herd of elephants forming what's called an "alert circle" around a wounded elephant. The older elephants—especially the matriarchs—stood shoulder to shoulder, forming a living wall to protect the vulnerable one inside. Any predator hoping to reach it would first have to get through several tons of protective mommas!

That's the kind of community we need, too—a "protective herd" of wise, loving women who will surround us, pray for us, and help us to heal. Scripture says, "Two are better than one, because they have a good return for their labor: if either of them falls down, one can help the other up" (Ecclesiastes 4:9-10).

As you heal and grow, ask God to help you find your tribe—the ones who will surround you in hard seasons. And in time, my prayer for you, sweet friend, is that you, too, will become that steady, protective presence for the next soul finding her way back to safety. That's the circle of healing, and it's exactly how God designed us to live.

Prayer:

Dear Father, help me to find my tribe—those who get me, who will protect me, and who will help me to grow into the woman You created me to be. As You heal my heart, help me also to reach back and lift up others on the path behind me. Amen.

Reflection:

Where are you at in building your tribe? Take a moment to reflect on your circles. Who encourages and protects you? Ask God to show you who belongs in your closest circle in this season or if you're further in your healing journey, how could you reach back to help the next sister walking this road behind you?

–Pause. Take a deep breath. What's one small step in your healing you can celebrate today?

Day 69

Who Can You Trust?
Identifying Safe People

"A friend loves at all times, and a brother is born for a time of adversity."

Proverbs 17:17

———Pause. Take a few deep breaths. Now rest—and abide in Him.———

After all you've survived—betrayal, abuse, or spiritual harm—you're going to need relationships that are truly safe. Healthy friendships are a vital piece of the healing process. While no relationship will be without flaws, there are some things to look for. You're not looking for fair-weather friends. You're looking for *all-weather* friends—those who stand beside you with their umbrella wide open, sheltering you from the storm and allowing you to do the same for them.

Safe friends see us as we are: messy, flawed, and in need of grace. They allow us to take off the mask, cry, stomp our feet, or be real in ways that can feel terrifying after what we've been through.

You're not looking for friends to carry all your burdens, or friends who dump all of theirs on you either. You're seeking mutuality: reciprocity, equal respect, care, kindness, and tenderness. These are the people you want to draw closer into your circle.

To help you identify them, I created an acronym: **SAFE FRIEND**[1]:

S – Safe: This person is safe, they don't try to hurt you, take advantage of you, gossip about you, invalidate you, or dismiss your feelings.

A – Authentic & Vulnerable: You can be messy around them—share your fears, failures, and insecurities without judgment.

F – Fosters Growth: They celebrate your successes, encourage you, and are a positive presence, there's no competition or jealousy.

E – Equal & Balanced: They help create a balanced mutual relationship with give-and-take; where both people invest time, energy, and care.

F – Faithful: They follow through on their promises and stand by you in hard times.

R – Respects Boundaries: They honor your limits and don't manipulate or guilt trip you.

I – Interested in You: They genuinely listen and show curiosity about your life.

E – Engages Honestly: They communicate truthfully, respectfully, speak truth with kindness; and conflict is handled constructively.

N – Nurtures Trust: They keep your secrets safe, and you can rely on them consistently.

D – Demonstrates Forgiveness: They apologize and make amends when they've done wrong, forgive when you do wrong, and can move forward with grace. In a safe relationship, you, too, will need to do the same.

You can use this acronym to help you think through who belongs in your circle—those who can help you feel safe again and grow healthier and stronger.

This isn't easy work. After betrayal or abuse, even recognizing safe people can feel scary. Your instincts have been wired for survival for a while now, so this is a normal feeling. You may not even trust your own "radar" anymore. So, take your time. Have grace on yourself.

Sweet friend, I'm cheering you on as you slowly rebuild your circle of trust, care, and connection. You've survived so much, you can do this, too, one safe friend at a time.

Prayer:

Dear Heavenly Father, it feels scary to know who to trust after being wounded so deeply. Help me grow in wisdom, discernment, and courage to trust myself to choose wisely. Please bring people into my life who have my best interests at heart and who will help me grow into the woman You created me to be. Amen.

Reflection:

Are the people in your support circle truly safe for you, and are they helping you grow and heal? If not, what small steps can you take to begin finding those who will?

–Pause. Take a deep breath. What's one small step in your healing you can celebrate today?

Day 70
Beware of Victim Blaming

"Each person is tempted when they are dragged away by their own evil desire and enticed. Then, after desire has conceived, it gives birth to sin; and sin, when it is full-grown, gives birth to death."
James 1:13-15

——*Pause. Take a few deep breaths. Now rest—and abide in Him.*——

Beloved, today I want to speak honestly about something many survivors face: victim blaming. It's painful and retraumatizing, so I want to offer what light I can to help you heal—and protect yourself if you encounter it.

Victim blaming is when someone blames the victim of abuse, adultery, or another person's addictions for the way the perpetrator behaves. Sometimes it's direct, but often it's subtle—so subtle it can slip past you in a conversation or in someone's "well-meaning" advice—only to leave a stinging sense of shame or doubt deep in your soul later on.

When a survivor shares her story and someone responds, "Well, have you prayed about it?" it can feel hurtful, as though the weight of what's happening is placed in your court to manage. While the person may not mean it in an unkind way, it implies that the survivor has not done enough spiritually to "fix" the situation. But often, by the time many survivors speak up, they've already prayed long and hard on bruised knees about their confusing marriage. Friend, I imagine you've prayed more in this season than most people will pray in their entire lives—because your life, your sanity, and maybe even your children's safety have depended on it.

Or someone may say to you, "I should really hear his side of the story," or ask, "What did you do to provoke him?" I've said this before, but it bears repeating: in cases of abuse or adultery, there is no "his side" that could ever change the reality of what you've experienced. Yes, we all make mistakes and have flaws, but that doesn't ever justify being abused or harmed. These kinds of comments can unintentionally imply that you somehow caused or invited the wrongdoing—and that simply isn't true.

At that point in the conversation, it's perfectly justified to politely end it—or, if it's someone you respect but you know they won't fully understand, to thank them for listening while firmly letting them know that you don't need anyone to speak with your husband about what you've shared in confidence. This isn't being rude; it's protecting yourself from further risk. Sometimes people need to hear things very clearly to grasp the full gravity of your situation.

Friend, the Bible is clear: Each person who sins does so of their own accord. No one makes them do it (James 1:13-15). No one forces them to act that way. You are not responsible for your husband's abuse, infidelity, or his addictions that lower his inhibitions and wreak havoc in your home.

Please hear me when I say this, and let it sink in deep: The weight of someone else's sin does not belong on your shoulders. You have already sacrificed enough. You are not to blame. You may still feel the ache, confusion, or fear—but you're free to release the guilt that was never yours to carry. Don't let anyone place that guilt back on your shoulders—God never asked you to carry it in the first place.

Prayer:

Dear Father, thank You for confirming to me that what others have unintentionally said is not true. Help me see even more clearly that I am not to blame for my husband's hurtful behavior. Guide me as I continue to work on my own healing and to be honest about my own patterns, while never carrying the blame for his. Amen.

Reflection:

Have you carried the blame for things that were not yours to carry? How does it feel to acknowledge that your husband's behaviors are his responsibility and not yours? Have you been retraumatized by the responses of others, and if so, how can you begin to release that weight and protect your heart?

–Pause. Take a deep breath. What's one small step in your healing you can celebrate today?

Day 71
When the Church Wounds

"Is this not the fast that I have chosen: to loose the bonds of wickedness, to undo the heavy burdens, to let the oppressed go free, and that you break every yoke?"

Isaiah 58:6

———*Pause. Take a few deep breaths. Now rest—and abide in Him.*———

Has your church been a haven of protection for you or added to your pain?

One of the first places many Christian women turn after infidelity, pornography use, or abuse is the church. And while that instinct is good, too often the response they receive is not. I've heard far too many stories where the church reinjures women, instead of helping them heal and find safety.

Now, I have worked with some churches that genuinely want to serve those who are suffering—and I pray yours is one of them. But in case it isn't, I want to gently prepare your heart for what to watch for.

Sometimes the damage happens not from cruelty, but ignorance, fear, or lack of being trained on how to respond to abuse or betrayal. While other leaders are so focused on saving marriages, they forget God values the safety and dignity of His children inside the marriage—first.

And sadly, then there *are* times when the very people you turn to for help are hiding the same sins or worse in their homes. That's hard to hear—but true. I share this because your safety matters far more than protecting the church's image. God never shields leaders who harm His people. Scripture warns, "Woe to the shepherds who destroy and scatter the sheep of My pasture!" (Jeremiah 23:1-2, Jeremiah 12:10, Matthew 18:6, Ezekiel 34:2-4).

So, what does spiritual harm, invalidation, or dismissal look like?

It might sound like, "just pray more," "forgive and forget," or "submit and trust God's timing"—without offering you protection or holding your spouse accountable. It might look like being told, "We need to understand his perspective too," as if the perspective of someone abusing you could honestly be trusted. That's like asking the fox to guard the henhouse.

It can come through spiritual assumptions, or blame disguised as advice or curiosity: "Maybe God is trying to teach you patience through this trial," or "Maybe if you tried being more available, he wouldn't look at pornography." Those words speak shame where compassion should have been offered.

Other times, leaders urge you to reconcile while it's still unsafe—twisting Scripture to say divorce is never an option, or that enduring harm might "win your husband over." Yet Jesus never asked anyone to stay in danger to prove their faithfulness.

You may even be told to "think of your children," as if having two parents—no matter how destructive one is—is always best. But as a wise counselor once told me, "One healthy parent is always better than a child growing up in a home where an unrepentant, abusive parent keeps causing harm."

Sometimes, church members struggle to believe your spouse could hurt anyone because he seems "so kind" and likeable in public. Or they want to protect his reputation because of his position. They might encourage secrecy, discourage calling the authorities, or warn you against "worldly counseling"—because "marriage issues *should* be private."

If this has been your experience, please hear me, dear friend: God is not like the people who failed to keep you safe. He never asks you to stay silent or in harm's way to protect His name. The only way to stop abuse is by naming it for what it is—and allowing real consequences to bring the truth into the light.

Because God's heart for His people has always been clear:

"Is this not the fast that I have chosen: to loose the bonds of wickedness, to undo the heavy burdens, *to let the oppressed go free, and that you break every yoke?*" (Isaiah 58:6, emphasis added).

Prayer:

Dear God, please show me who is safe to share my story with, and give me wisdom and courage as I begin to speak my truth. Please also heal the hurt I feel from those who did not protect me. Amen.

Reflection:

Reflect on who might be safe to share with, and consider preparing what you will say beforehand. If you've already shared and been wounded by the response, take time to explore what other churches, counselors, or communities in your area might provide a safer, more compassionate space for your healing.

–Pause. Take a deep breath. What's one small step in your healing you can celebrate today?

Day 72
Finding Wise Counsel

"Where there is no counsel, the people fall; but in the multitude of counselors there is safety."
Proverbs 11:14

———*Pause. Take a few deep breaths. Now rest—and abide in Him.*———

In some Christian circles I've been a part of, seeking professional counseling or coaching is treated as taboo. I've even heard people say "All we need is the Bible, prayer, and our relationship with God and that can fix anything."

While I *wholeheartedly* agree that God is the greatest Healer— and that He could, if He chose, heal our hearts without any outside help (just as He could also miraculously heal cancer or any other terminal disease)—most often, He chooses to work through skilled, compassionate people to help us on our journey to wholeness.

I feel certain that the same people who insist on relying solely on prayer and Scripture wouldn't say that if they broke a leg in a car accident and couldn't walk. They'd most likely see a doctor to set their leg and eventually work with a physical therapist to regain strength, so they could walk again. Yet somehow, when it comes to healing our minds and hearts, many treat it differently.

Scripture itself says, "Where there is no counsel, the people fall; but *in the multitude of counselors there is safety*" (Proverbs 11:14, NKJV, emphasis added).

Dear friend, if your heart and soul are languishing from the devastation in your marriage, seeking help is not a sin—it's wise. It's biblical. The same goes for your children as they try to navigate this difficult season.

There are many Christian counselors, coaches, ministries, domestic violence shelters, and even some ministers who can help. The caveat is to do some vetting. Make sure the help you seek is trauma- and abuse-informed, because if you're here reading this, it's likely you've experienced one or both. Not every secular *or* Christian counselor, coach, pastor, or ministry is trained to help navigate abuse, betrayal, or spousal addiction. But many are, so simply do your research.

Look for someone who doesn't minimize your experiences, has the wisdom to guide you, prioritizes your safety, and reinforces your right to make your own choices.

You may feel isolated—by your husband's control, his addictions, or the shame and exhaustion you've been carrying. Trauma can cloud our thinking and cause us to withdraw—but having someone in your corner helps you sift through the fog and gain clarity. An objective perspective can help, especially when you're too close to the chaos to see things clearly yourself.

Scripture and prayer are powerful, absolutely. But as a survivor myself, I can attest that waiting for God to speak while you stay in chaos and isolation can leave you frozen. I spent nearly four years in analysis paralysis, waiting for God to tell me *exactly* what to do. Hope felt distant, and God seemed silent—but He wasn't.

What I couldn't see then was that God had already placed a wise Christian counselor and safe support groups in my life—and *they* had been speaking His truths to me all along. I just couldn't recognize it at first, because I had learned to spiritualize everything. I had been taught to treat every decision as though it required a divine sign and to distrust every feeling I had, because I had repeatedly heard in sermons and teachings that my heart is "wicked." And while Scripture does say the heart can be deceitful, that message, taken in isolation, overlooks the many other biblical principles that show we *can* trust ourselves, because God grants us wisdom when we ask for it. So when God used ordinary people to speak wisdom, I dismissed it as "not being spiritual enough," without even realizing what I was doing.

But their guidance was God's provision. They were the voices He used to lead me through the fog. And my husband's continued harmful behaviors were the "sign" I had been begging God for; it just took time for me to accept that his ongoing patterns *were* my answer.

God had already been showing me the truth long before I was ready to admit it. It was through hearing other women's stories and having wisdom shared with me in the confidentiality of a counseling room that I realized God hadn't been silent at all. I could hear Him more clearly than ever, because I finally stopped spiritualizing what He had already made plain.

Prayer:

Dear God, please guide me to those who understand my situation and are equipped to help me. Give me Your peace on this journey and clarity for my steps forward. Amen.

Reflection:

Are you already working with someone who is helping you? If so, what lessons or insights can you put into action? If not, what steps could you take to find the support you need?

–Pause. Take a deep breath. What's one small step in your healing you– can celebrate today?

Day 73
From Surviving to Thriving

"Being confident of this very thing, that He who has begun a good work in you will complete it until the day of Jesus Christ."

Philippians 1:6

——*Pause. Take a few deep breaths. Now rest—and abide in Him.*——

Just like a butterfly that experiences a multi-phased transformation—from a caterpillar to a soaring creature—this is our story, too. When we're in survival mode, we're like the caterpillar—solely focused on staying alive—eating, surviving, just getting through the day. This mirrors stage one of Restoring Safety.

But as you move through the stages, I-Investing in stability, S-Speaking your truth, your focus begins to shift, much like the butterfly preparing to emerge. And now you're about to enter the final stage: Emerging Stronger.

This stage will invite you to live differently. Just as the caterpillar must learn to fly, so will you. But when it first leaves its cocoon, its wings are wet, crumpled, and fragile—not yet strong enough to soar. It's in a vulnerable, uncomfortable state.

You, too, may feel that same vulnerability now. You've endured so much—and I hope you've also begun to heal. But understand, the transition from surviving to thriving can still feel shaky.

Living in survival mode meant existing on high alert because your mind and body were convinced danger or uncertainty was around every corner. And when this happens our life shrinks to a single purpose: staying alive, both physically and emotionally. That leaves little time for joy, rest, creativity, or connection with others.

Physically, this constant state of fight or flight shows up as exhaustion, sleep disturbances, digestive issues, lack of focus, impulsiveness, aggressiveness, struggling to keep up with the basics of everyday life, and feeling foggy-headed. Even making the simplest choice can feel overwhelming.

After long seasons of hyper-vigilance, calm can actually feel foreign. Chaos becomes our baseline. So, when we leave it behind, our trauma-wired brains often seek out excitement to fill the void. Your body is no longer fueled by the cortisol and adrenaline that once kept you "alive." Our bodies become acclimated to those stress hormones because they provide a rush, so when they end, much like an addiction we may even experience withdrawals.

Your body may not know how to stop living on high alert. When life suddenly grows quiet, the stillness can feel dull or boring, and without meaning to, your mind and body begin to recreate the very chaos you left behind.

You might overreact to ordinary problems or treat small issues like a crisis. You may have an oversensitive startle response or have a hard time interpreting others' actions and view them as threatening when they aren't. Your past experiences can cloud each interaction, making it hard to gauge intentions accurately.

Even a simple comment might feel like "fighting" words—because in your world, it always has been. This can leave you jumpy, defensive, or acting in ways that surprise you. In response, many trauma survivors try to control everything around them, hoping to quiet their internal chaos and racing thoughts. We might micromanage, overwork, or stop trusting others.

Boundaries may become a challenge again—because we desperately need other people's approval to feel OK. It can be our misguided way of seeking worth through how others see us.

Coming out of survival mode, much like the butterfly emerging from its cocoon, takes time. It's a gentle process of retraining your mind and body to trust that it's safe. Treat yourself with compassion; this isn't easy. Don't forget to rest, nourish your body, practice self-care, and stillness, and take time to breathe—deeply and often.

Over time, as you repeat these rhythms, your body will move from constant alertness to being present and give you the freedom to truly live again. That's the place God has prepared for you—a place of safety and deep abiding in His peace.

Don't be afraid to go through the mess to get there, sweet friend. You can be "confident of this very thing, that He who has begun a good work in you will complete it." He will never leave you (Philippians 1:6, NKJV).

Prayer:

Dear God, please help me to recognize the moments when my mind or body slip back into chaos. Teach me how to calm my nervous system and rest in the safety You've provided. Help me to release old patterns of fear and control and to trust the peace I now have. Thank You for continuing to heal and transform me from the inside out.

Reflection:

In what ways are you still living as if danger is near? What small nurturing actions can help remind your nervous system, that you are safe now?

–Pause. Take a deep breath. What's one small step in your healing you– can celebrate today?

Emerging Stronger

Rising Higher

You have now walked through restoring safety, investing in stability, and speaking your truth. Now comes the season of emerging—stronger. Just as the butterfly emerges from its hidden season of transformation, fragile at first, but soon confident and strong, you, too, can rise above and find the freedom God created you for. Freedom from the cycles of hurt and pain, freedom from shame, and freedom from pretending things are OK when they're not.

In this final part of our journey together, you'll be able to reflect on how you've grown, embrace your new identity in Christ, and step into the hope-filled future God has waiting for you. I hope you will discover new joy, renewed strength, and the courage to live with purpose. Emerging stronger won't mean that all of your past or even pain will disappear, but it *can mean* that you continue allowing God to transform your story into one of freedom and lasting peace.

Day 74

It's Never Too Late to Start Writing a New Chapter

*"Fear not, for I am with you; be not dismayed,
for I am your God. I will strengthen you, yes, I will help you,
I will uphold you with My righteous right hand."*
Isaiah 41:10 (NKJV)

———*Pause. Take a few deep breaths. Now rest—and abide in Him.*———

Maybe you've felt stuck or paralyzed in making decisions lately. Sometimes we struggle to move forward because of the pain in our past or because the present feels like a tie that binds us, holding us back. Don't be afraid to lean into those hard places in your soul.

It's easy to become stuck in loops of ruminating thoughts or in the "what ifs" of life. This can make you feel alone, as if everyone else has it together—except you. But you're not alone.

The pages of the Bible are filled with men and women who had hard pasts. I heard a beautiful message at church years ago that I want to share a paraphrased portion of, because I believe it could bless you like it did me.

As Christians, we often focus on the story of how Jesus came into this world—a story of a baby, and a soon-to-be King born in a manger. Rightfully so—it changed history. But I want to guide your attention even further back in the story of Jesus. It might seem like a paradox, but I've found that looking at our history can often help us move forward with more confidence.

Before Jesus came into this world, four women played an important role in paving the way. We've discussed two of them in earlier devotions, but not the other two. We don't hear much about these women, but I think their stories could be significant for you as you go through your journey toward healing.

These four women were part of the direct lineage of Christ. And their stories were anything but tidy. In fact, they were really quite messy.

Tamar, Rahab, Ruth, and Bathsheba. Four women who weren't exactly esteemed in their day. They each had hard and complicated stories. Maybe you feel like your story isn't tidy either. Mine certainly hasn't been. If this is you, I hope this brings you peace and clarity as it did for me.

Tamar was forgotten and set aside after the death of her first husband, and then again after the death of her second husband. She was left in limbo by her father-in-law, Judah, who according to tradition, was to provide his next son, as her husband. Instead, he wronged Tamar, which left her penniless. But Tamar took action, changing the course of her story—and ultimately, the story of generations to come (Genesis 38).

In our way of thinking, this may seem like a messy twist, but in God's eyes, Tamar's pursuit of justice placed her in the lineage of Jesus.

Rahab was a prostitute in a marginalized society, and she was also a Canaanite—who were enemies of the Israelites. To say the least, Rahab was far from esteemed in either society. Yet, she changed her story when she bravely stood up for God and His people. In doing so, she became the mother of Boaz, placing her also in the direct line of Jesus (Joshua 2, Matthew 1:5).

Then there's Ruth, a Moabite whose culture was also at odds with the Israelites. Her story is filled with grief—losing her husband, her brother-in-law, her father-in-law, and eventually her own people. After so much loss, Ruth made what must have been a frightening decision that changed her story. She chose God's path instead of clinging to her past. As a result, she became the wife of Boaz and the great-grandmother of King David. Once again, another woman who changed the course of her story by stepping into God's plan.

And finally, Bathsheba. Her story is one of heartache turned into triumph. King David sexually forced himself on Bathsheba, and then killed her husband, Uriah. Trauma upon trauma. If anyone could claim to be a victim of injustice, it was Bathsheba. Yet, she didn't let her story end there. She used her position as the king's wife to ensure that her son—not David's other sons—would become the next king.

By doing so, she secured her place in the heritage of the ultimate King of the universe. And God honored her for this. In Matthew 1:6, God calls out David's sins against her, referring to Bathsheba as "her who had been the wife of Uriah." God didn't let her pain go unnoticed. He called it out, for generations to witness, and for centuries to come.

God sees your pain and your past too. It has not gone unnoticed. God honors your bravery to change your story by changing the steps you take going forward. You don't have to stay stuck in the hurt of your past. God has a plan and a future for you that can change the ending of your story—just as He did for these four women.

Don't let your past or current struggles define your future—God doesn't. Now is the time to begin rewriting your story and taking different steps in order to create a better future.

Prayer:

Dear Heavenly Father, thank You for the stories of the brave women in the Bible and how You honored them. Please lift me up also, as I seek to take courageous strides in this next chapter of my life. Amen.

Reflection:

What do the stories of these four women and others in the Bible speak to your heart? Take a moment to reflect or journal how their stories might influence your own.

–Pause. Take a deep breath. What's one small step in your healing you can celebrate today?

Day 75
Don't Let Anyone Steal Your Joy

"And I will restore to you the years that the locust hath eaten."
Joel 2:25, KJV

——*Pause. Take a few deep breaths. Now rest—and abide in Him.*——

I remember the first time my son and I ate a meal in our own home and didn't feel the normal tension. We were sitting at the kitchen table, and something silly was said that struck us as funny—and for the first time in a long time, we both laughed, long and hard, until our bellies hurt.

The laughter was contagious, and the more we laughed, the more I felt a deep sense of freedom. And then my son looked at me and said something that spoke volumes: "Mom, we never could've done that before."

We *wouldn't* have done that before because we were too afraid. We never knew if laughter would be seen as too silly or irreverent, and then the tension—or a long lecture filled with frustration or anger—would follow, leaving our meal ruined. It was a scene that replayed many times in our home.

And that's when it hit me. I *never* wanted either of us to go back to a place where we weren't free to laugh—free to experience joy—*free to be ourselves*—whatever that meant in that season. That day, I made a promise to myself: I would never again let anyone steal my joy.

I've learned that our joy comes from the Lord—it's a God-given gift, and He would never ask us to hand it over to someone else's dysfunction.

Our joy can be stolen by patterns of manipulation, emotional control, gaslighting, addiction, betrayal—all the things that cause us to walk on eggshells, trying to predict the next outburst or decipher what's true or not true. When we live in confusion, chaos, and deep betrayal, our soul starts to shrink. Survival mode keeps us so focused on getting by that we lose the ability to truly be present—to notice beauty, to laugh, or to experience peace.

Joy can even be stolen from within. When we spend all our energy trying to change someone else, picking up after their mistakes, or carrying the weight of their addictions and issues, we become exhausted rather than alive. Bitterness builds when we hold onto what we cannot control, and even the blessings God gives us can begin to feel heavy under the weight of resentment.

But, friend, that's not the abundant life that God has promised you. Jesus tells us in John 10:10 that He came that you and I could have life—and have it *abundantly*. That includes joy—and laughter! That includes the freedom to fully be who God made you to be.

God didn't create us to live under the microscope of someone else or to merely survive the fallout of their sins. He made us to live in His freedom and grace. We are called to seek *His* will—not the approval of someone who uses control, blame shifting, or shame to keep us small and silent.

Dear friend, are you free to speak your truth, to share your opinions honestly—or are you shrinking to keep the peace? Please know that if you can't share how you feel or tell your husband how you've been hurt without fear of retribution, that is not God's best for you—or your children.

Children need to be able to express themselves, so they can develop without fear. And just as importantly, you, sweet friend, deserve that same freedom to be seen, known, and loved for who you truly are.

God loves the real you, not the version of you that pleases everyone else to keep the peace. Don't allow your God-given identity to be chipped away by someone else's idea of who you *should* be or by the constant struggle to keep a broken relationship together on your own.

While Joel 2:25 was originally spoken to Israel after their own sin, I believe it also holds a tender message for those who have been deeply wounded by the sins of others, "I will restore the years that the locusts have eaten."

Dear friend, I don't know if your restoration will happen inside or outside of your marriage—but I do know this: God wants to give you beauty for ashes, laughter for tears, and hope where hopelessness once lived. He promises to do this as you trust Him and you focus on living the abundant life He has for you.

Prayer:

Dear Father, some days I feel like I've lost my joy. I can't even remember what truly brings me happiness, because for so long pain and confusion surrounding my marriage has consumed my heart. Please lift my head and help me to be fully present. Restore my laughter, renew my identity in You, and teach me how to guard the joy You've placed within me. I commit to never letting anyone steal that joy again. Amen.

Reflection:

What have been your "joy thieves"? What's one small step you can take to reclaim your peace and joy this week?

–Pause. Take a deep breath. What's one small step in your healing you can celebrate today?

Day 76

Lost and Found in the Wilderness: Walking in Dignity Again

"But You, O Lord, are a shield for me,
My glory and the One who lifts up my head."
Psalm 3:3, NKJV

———*Pause. Take a few deep breaths. Now rest—and abide in Him.*———

While out hiking one day, I got lost—really lost. Every path I tried felt wrong, so I turned around and tried again, each time becoming more frustrated. It had already been one of *those* days.

I'd gone for a hike with my dog, Scout, hoping to reconnect with God. But truthfully, I was just numb. I had just come back from a hard summer, one that was supposed to be my "healing journey" after years of holding everything together through separation, divorce, and starting my private practice. My son and I had packed up, bought a shiny new RV, and headed out west for a few months, where I hoped we would finally have a season to refresh.

From day one, it all went sideways. The RV broke down. Then came the carbon monoxide leak that sent us to the ER. Just when

I thought I could take a breath, a drunk driver hit us and fled the scene, meaning no insurance to cover our totaled vehicle. We were grateful to be alive, but my savings had dwindled, my hope felt crushed, and now months later, we were back east staying with family, waiting on a resolution on the RV so we could move forward.

So, there I was, lost in the woods, trying to heal from my *attempts at healing*. I finally hit a wall. I flopped down on the damp dirt, with a leash tied around my waist to an impatient pup tugging nearby.

Just then, my phone picked up a signal long enough for one email to come through—from an attorney who offered to help our RV issue pro-bono: "There's nothing more I can do. The manufacturer won't respond."

That was it—the last straw on my already weary camel's back. And it all came tumbling out, right there in the woods. It wasn't pretty—ugly crying, dripping nose, and all. Looking back, if some poor soul had wandered off the trail right then, they probably would've thought I'd lost it completely!

Out it came: "God, I have no clue which way to go—now or even in life! Do You even see me or care anymore?"

And suddenly, I thought of the story of Hagar—alone in the desert, sitting across from Ishmael, running out of water and hope. OK, so in my case, Ishmael was Scout, and I imagine my blubbering pity party was far less graceful. But I felt her desperation.

Maybe you've heard the saying, "If you're hysterical, it's historical." That was me. This *was* historical. My trauma had been buried under busyness. But now the betrayal, the losses, the exhaustion—it all demanded to be seen.

And in that release, I had a revelation. God brought the lesson home. Hagar wasn't Sarah. She wasn't the mother of the promised child. *But she was someone to God.* He saw her mistreatment. He heard the cry of her son. He met her in her despair. And then, He opened her eyes to see a well that had been there all along.

Concern. Care. Provision. He promised her despair would *not* have the final word.

He didn't erase her suffering, but He did restore her dignity.

And right there in my own wilderness moment, I realized the same was true for me. God saw me. He saw my mistreatment, the injustice, my losses, my trying so hard to survive. And though He didn't erase the pain, He met me in it—and began restoring my dignity. And, dear friend, He will do the same for you.

Maybe that's the thing about our breaking points—they don't look "holy," but sometimes they're the holiest moments of all.

Prayer:

Dear Heavenly Father, help me to trust that You see me, too. And help me to grieve what I've lost while You continue restoring my dignity. Just as You did for Hagar, please use my story for Your glory also. Amen.

Reflection:

What makes you feel most overwhelmed right now? When was the last time you let yourself cry or express your frustration freely? What did that release feel like?

What does "restoring dignity" mean to you? And what small, tangible step could help you move toward that restoration?

—Pause. Take a deep breath. What's one small step in your healing you can celebrate today?

Day 77

When God Slows Us Down to Give us Hope

"Then God opened her eyes, and she saw a well of water. And she went and filled the skin with water, and gave the lad a drink."
Genesis 21:19

———*Pause. Take a few deep breaths. Now rest—and abide in Him.*———

Remember Hagar—and the story I shared with you in yesterday's devotional? The truth is, my day didn't end there. I was still lost, tear-streaked, and weary when God began to speak something deeper into my heart.

No sooner had I found comfort in the first revelation about Hagar's story than another thought hit me: "But why can't I be Sarah?" I remember grumbling through my tears. "Why do some of us have to be Hagar—the one left behind, the one mistreated, the one who feels unseen?"

And there on the dirt, in the woods, His response came—not harsh, not audible, but steady and kind, in that still, small nudging of the heart.

"Dear daughter, if Hagar hadn't gone through what she did, where would you draw your strength from now? And what if, because of your story, another worn down soul finds comfort through the healing you'll one day share? I wasn't the cause of Hagar's misfortune—Sarah and Abraham's misguided choices were. And I'm not the author of your pain or confusion either. But just as I was with Hagar, I am with you now. I see you, and I will not leave you in the middle of your struggle."

That moment undid me—but this time in a gentler way.

I realized I had been so busy, that *I* was the reason I hadn't been able to connect with God. Yes, I had been praying, but I hadn't paused long enough to truly listen. I needed to get lost that day because it was the only way God could help me see what I had been missing.

God hadn't forgotten me. He wasn't distant—He was waiting.

And then that still, small voice whispered again: "Because I use the Hagars, too. I see you. You're not done yet. You have much to live for—and My provisions are never late."

As I sat there in the stillness, I began to see what He was showing me: Even the heroes of faith came from messy families and complicated stories. Not every marriage works. Not every child turns out as hoped. Not every family looks like two kids, a two-car garage, and a glowingly happy life. And, apparently, that's always been true—even in Abraham's family tree!

I'm still floored by how God meets us in our messiest moments—when the tears are raw, when we don't have answers, when the path looks nothing like we planned.

Friend, don't be afraid to let God slow you down too. He may lead you to a quiet place—not to punish you, but, to remind you that He still sees you, still loves you, and still has a promise for your future, too.

Prayer:

Dear Lord, maybe You're speaking to me, showing me that the place where I feel lost is exactly where You want to meet me and reveal a well of provision I couldn't see before. Please show me, speak to me, and guide me. Help me to trust in Your timing, not my own. Amen.

Reflection:

Is God inviting you to stop running and to rest in His care today? Where do you feel lost, confused, or too busy to see the way forward?

–Pause. Take a deep breath. What's one small step in your healing you– can celebrate today?

Day 78

Write the Vision and Learn to Dream Again

"Write the vision and make it plain... For the vision is yet for an appointed time; but at the end it will speak... Though it tarries, wait for it; because it will surely come, it will not tarry.'"

Habakkuk 2:2-3, NKJV

——— *Pause. Take a few deep breaths. Now rest—and abide in Him.* ———

Has God begun to stir a vision in your heart, but you hesitate because of self-doubt or those old, familiar voices whispering, "you can't"?

When I was homeschooling my son, I probably said this one quote, by Henry Ford, far too often (to this day, he'll tell you it's not his favorite!): "Whether you think you can or think you can't, you're right." What we allow to roll around in our heads is often exactly what unfolds in our life.

But I love how God reframes our fearful "I'll never be good enough" moments. In Isaiah 54:4 He says, "Do not be afraid; you will not be put to shame. Do not fear disgrace; you will not be humiliated. You will forget the shame of your youth and remember no more the reproach of your widowhood."

Do you hear the strength and determination in that verse? I do. Then listen to the next verse, "For your Maker is your husband—the Lord Almighty is his name—the Holy One of Israel is your Redeemer."

Friend, when God is the One helping us to write our story, He stands behind His work. He redeems what feels lost or broken and invites us to dream again—because He knows our next chapter is waiting.

In Habakuk 2:2-3 we're told to,

> Write the vision and make *it* plain... For the vision *is* yet for an appointed time...Though it tarries, wait for it; because it will surely come.

God knows we wrestle with doubt—I believe that's why He asks us to write our vision down. He is calling us to make a commitment to it and writing it down makes that feel more real—it becomes a plan we aren't as likely to forget.

Years ago, I did exactly that. After praying, for what felt like a long season, for God to use my pain for a greater purpose, He began to reveal glimpses of His plan. Each time He did, I would jot them down in my notes app on my phone.

Then one day, I decided to get *serious* about writing down my vision. Determined, I drove to the local craft store, bought one of those oversized presentation boards (because, friend, I was going to dream big after all!) and started pouring everything that God had been showing me onto that huge board.

When I stepped back, I surprised even myself. I actually began to see a path forming—a ministry to help women, a book to speak into their pain, and a practice to walk alongside others in their healing journey.

For a while, I kept that giant board in the back of my closet. And whenever I felt discouraged or like the vision was "tarrying,"

I'd wrangle that big board out, prop it up, and remind myself to keep going.

Eventually, I realized the board was, well, a "bit much." So I upgraded to a clear trifold menu folder and transferred my hopes and dreams onto letter-sized paper instead. Much easier to pull out—and a lot less dramatic than wrestling with the presentation board every time I needed inspiration!

Dear friend, God has amazing things in your future. He wants you to dream again. Even if you're unsure what that looks like, you can start by asking Him to show you—and allow your purpose to unfold as you pray.

Purpose isn't always one big thing—it's often many small things that use your gifts, your experiences, and yes, even your pain. And our purpose can grow, shift, or change over time.

Allow God to take those years of hardships and trials and turn them into your testimony. He is still the God who transforms pain into purpose.

Prayer:

Dear Father, please reveal my next steps toward the purpose You have for me now. Your Word is like a lamp unto my feet; I understand if I don't see the whole path at once. I just need enough light for the next step, and Lord, I'm ready to take it. Amen.

Reflection:

Take some time to pray and ask God to reveal His purposes for your life. As He does, keep a piece of paper or journal nearby to capture the dreams, callings, or stirrings you sense may be a part of your future. This takes intentionality—so, if possible, create moments to linger in His Word, to pause, and to be still enough to hear His gentle nudging.

–Pause. Take a deep breath. What's one small step in your healing you– can celebrate today?

Day 79
Financial Independence with God's Wisdom

*"If you are faithful in little things,
you will be faithful in large ones."*
Luke 16:10, NLT

———*Pause. Take a few deep breaths. Now rest—and abide in Him.*———

After my divorce, I became painfully aware that I had been avoiding my finances. And when I say avoiding, I mean like the plague. I wasn't reckless with money—I simply wasn't aware of what I was spending.

By the time the divorce finally came, I felt like I had to hit the ground running. I had already been separated for nearly four years—praying, waiting, hoping for change that never came. During those years, I grieved, processed, worked with my counselor, and sat in numerous support groups. I had been healing. But the one thing I hadn't done was learn how to manage money. I *thought* I knew how.

What I didn't realize was that I needed to heal my *relationship* with money—and my fearful mindset and habits reflected that truth.

While I thought I had always managed money well during my marriage, I began to see that since I was only given a small allowance, didn't handle the bills, and wasn't the one working—I didn't actually have much *to* manage. Suddenly, I was doing all of those things—*and so much more*! I was and still am grateful for the support I received during and after the divorce, but even that—in the economy we were in—was barely enough to survive.

During the separation, I was a stay-at-home mom as my son finished high school. My work was inconsistent, and the bills still needed to be paid. To say I was scrappy in those years would be an understatement. I sold so many belongings at yard sales that my son must have wondered if we'd have beds left to sleep on!

Then one day, God slowed me down and spoke to my busy (and weary) heart: "If you're faithful in little things, you will be faithful in large ones."

I didn't hear this as shame, but as truth. I had been running so fast that I hadn't slowed down to honestly look at my finances or even create a budget. That's when I decided—the buck (no pun intended) would stop there. But I also had compassion for myself. I began to understand that my financial avoidance was not a moral failure to feel guilty about, but rather a trauma response.

I hired a money coach and started learning better habits, working through my fears and scarcity mindset. For many of us, who have known financial control or instability, the topic of money can feel loaded—full of shame or fear. But God's wisdom invites us to see money not as a measure of worth or happiness, but as a tool for freedom and peace. Healing your relationship with money is a part of your overall healing.

Maybe you, too, need to pause and assess. This step, like all the others on your healing journey, is important. Name what's happening with your finances. Take a bold, honest look. Are you over-spending, or are you penny-pinching and leaving no space for some spontaneity and joy?

What would it look like to trust God with this part of your life—not just for provision, but for wisdom?

I hope, as you're able, that you can rest in the truth that "God will meet all your needs according to His riches in glory in Christ Jesus" (Philippians 4:19).

Prayer:

Dear Heavenly Father, I have been busy, and I haven't slowed down to think about my relationship with money. I pray not only for Your provisions in this hard season, but also for Your wisdom to help me see any areas that need my attention. Thank You for Your love and compassion as I continue to grow and learn, and help me to have this for myself as well. Amen.

Reflection:

What areas of your finances could use more attention—your budget, your savings, your spending habits, or your mindset about money? Write them down and begin thinking through a few small steps you can take to address them.

–Pause. Take a deep breath. What's one small step in your healing you– can celebrate today?

Day 80
Creatively Healing the Soul

"Sing to Him a new song; play skillfully with a shout of joy."
Psalm 33:3, NKJV

——*Pause. Take a few deep breaths. Now rest—and abide in Him.*——

Trauma is a thief. It numbs parts of us that God wants to awaken. It lessens our ability to be present, diminishes imagination, and steals our joy. Healing means inviting God to breathe life back into those quiet, hidden places again. Part of restoration—in mind, body, and soul—is reclaiming the things trauma stole from you.

This may mean doing something completely new, or rekindling something you once enjoyed or were passionate about. You might find creative expression—painting, music, photography, or crafts—to be healing. Or you may find healing through sensory activities that are more hands-on, such as gardening, cooking, baking, or decorating.

For others, body-based creativity—like a walk in nature, stretching, moving to music—can help you feel at peace in your body again. Restorative play, like puzzles, knitting, sewing, building, or scrapbooking, can also help. And storytelling—journaling, poetry, writing letters, or sharing your testimony—can turn pain into purpose.

I remember listening to a podcast by author Asheritah Ciuciu, and she said something that struck me: Experiencing awe has been studied and proven to be deeply healing for the soul and helps to restore joy. An awe-inspiring scene invites us to pause, notice God's beauty, and reconnect with the wonder of life. God has put so many different things in our path to help us heal.

There's no one-size-fits all approach—it's about what feels right for you in this season. Allow God to inspire you to engage in activities that heal your mind, move your body, and reawaken your senses. He delights as you rediscover joy, beauty, and His presence.

Engaging your creative mind isn't about what you produce or accomplish; it's about relearning how to be present in your own life and allowing God to restore joy within you, so His beauty can take root in your heart again.

Prayer:

Dear Father, I've spent too much time watching life from the sidelines. While others have been out making memories, trauma has kept me exhausted, isolated, and afraid. Please show me ways I can re-engage with the world around me. Open my eyes to see Your beauty again and help me to experience it with wonder as You continue to heal my heart. Amen.

Reflection:

What are some activities that could help you be more present and truly enjoy your life again? Are there hobbies you once enjoyed but have set aside that you would like to start again? Or are there new things you'd like to try—a walking club, a pottery class, or maybe building a raised garden bed?

–Pause. Take a deep breath. What's one small step in your healing you can celebrate today?

Day 81
Healthy Friendships Ahead

"God sets the lonely in families,
He leads out the prisoners with singing."
Psalm 68:6

——*Pause. Take a few deep breaths. Now rest—and abide in Him.*——

Sometimes we build walls so high that we brick ourselves in. It may feel natural to isolate yourself because relationships still feel like a risk—but try not to. God invites us to keep growing and healing, and a part of that growth comes through staying connected in safe communities and with safe people. While it's true we are wounded in relationships, it's also true we are *healed* in them.

Scripture says that "God sets the lonely in families, he leads out the prisoners with singing;" (Psalm 68:6). Isn't that beautiful? God sees your loneliness, and His heart is for you to belong.

Sometimes that belonging comes through new friendships; sometimes it begins with simply learning to trust again—with Him and with yourself. If your church isn't safe right now, seek out one that is. If there are friendships that, deep down, you know aren't healthy, it's OK to let go. You're not being unkind—you're choosing peace. Remember, your goal is to *thrive*, not merely survive.

God desires to nurture you with loyal, life-giving connections and will walk with you as you take steps toward those. Your circle may be smaller now, and that's OK—that can happen as we rebuild and heal. Maybe you've had to release those who couldn't walk this journey with you. Most people only have a few close friends—what truly matters is depth, not breadth.

As you keep healing, continue to strengthen your existing friendships. Also, try to notice the openings God provides for new relationships—a kind conversation, a shared laugh, an unexpected sense of comfort with someone new.

Sweet friend, keep your heart open, even just a little. Healing for you may mean many new friends or a few—but it definitely means seeking out the ones who see you and love you as you truly are. And while you wait, please know that you're never alone in God's care. He is the friend who sticks closer than any other.

Prayer:

Dear God, please guide me to safe friendships and community that can nurture my healing and growth. Thank You for being my closest and most faithful friend. Help me to connect with You on a deeper level, and to trust that You will never leave me. Amen.

Reflection:

Where might you be able to start connecting with others? Are there communities or people who make you feel seen, supported, and valued? How can you start building those connections while protecting your heart?

–Pause. Take a deep breath. What's one small step in your healing you can celebrate today?

Day 82
Intimacy with Wisdom

*"Above all else, guard your heart,
for everything you do flows from it."*
Proverbs 4:23

―――*Pause. Take a few deep breaths. Now rest―and abide in Him.*―――

At a very young age, before I knew the Lord, I walked through some pretty dark valleys. I endured years of identity-shattering bullying in junior high and high school that led to anorexia, which in turn, contributed to developing epilepsy. By sixteen, an older man at work took advantage of me sexually, and in search of worth and belonging, I began seeking out unhealthy relationships. By seventeen, I was pregnant; by eighteen, I was a young bride.

To say that life was hard during those years would be an understatement.

That marriage was chaotic beyond measure. Though I loved him, it was terrifying at times. He was an alcoholic, and one night, I found myself at the other end of a gun—not out of malice, but foolishness fueled by alcohol. Thankfully, I knew it was time to leave.

But leaving didn't heal me. Because at that point in my life "normal" felt like dysfunction. I turned right around and carried years of trauma into another relationship, which ended just as dramatically after unraveling lies, fraud, and this time a hidden addiction. All of which took place before I ever left my twenties. It wasn't until I found the Lord *and* a good counselor that I began to heal.

Yet, no one, not even my counselor, warned me of something subtle but dangerous. Trauma survivors often minimize bad behavior in future relationships because in comparison to our earlier experiences we set the bar low for what "normal" should feel like.

Years later, I thought I had finally found true love. But as a new Christian, I was extremely naïve. I believed Christians didn't have problems, and that my faith meant marriage would naturally be good, because God was a part of it.

I began noticing small concerning behaviors, but they were inconsistent. So, I brushed them off: "At least he doesn't drink, or do drugs," I told myself. It was nothing like I had lived through before. And though I had been in counseling, my self-worth was still fragile. I thought I was lucky that *any* man would want me after all I had been through. Beloved, don't believe this lie—you are worthy of respect and a healthy relationship, no matter your past.

I tolerated unkindness, anger, and confusion. At the time, it seemed minor compared to my past, but over time it grew into chaos. For trauma survivors, this is common: We compare, we minimize, and we risk repeating unhealthy patterns that present themselves in a different package.

This can happen in a new relationship, but even in your current marriage, especially if the most visible dangers have stopped (drinking, physical abuse, cheating), suddenly emotional harm and disrespect can begin to surface. Recognizing that doesn't mean you failed, it means you're seeing things clearly now.

Now this isn't everyone's story; I know many stories of survivors who remarry *wonderful*, healthy men. Because there *are* truly good men out there. But I share my experience because I want to give you what wasn't given to me—wisdom.

Dear friend, whether you're still in your marriage or have left, give yourself *plenty* of time to find yourself again. Don't be afraid to do the work needed to heal those deep, sometimes hidden places in your heart, before you give it to someone new—or re-enter your marriage without ensuring trust has been earned.

Scripture cautions us, "Above all else, guard your heart, for everything you do flows from it" (Proverbs 4:23).

Healing isn't just about surviving the past; it's also about cultivating discernment and self-worth so that, whether you stay in your marriage or are in a new relationship after divorce, you can recognize both the good *and* the warning signs.

Beloved, God's ultimate goal is to heal your heart. You don't have to rush into any relationship, until your heart and soul have found true healing in the One who will never harm you.

Prayer:

Dear Father, You see where I'm at. Relationships have been confusing. Please help me not to minimize what's unhealthy or harmful and give me the wisdom to see clearly. Teach me how to trust again, Lord, when it's truly safe to do so. Amen.

Reflection:

Take some time to learn what healthy love looks like. For a list of red flags and green flags in dating or marriage see the Resource section in the back of the book.

–Pause. Take a deep breath. What's one small step in your healing you can celebrate today?

Day 83

Repairers of the Breach, Building the Old Waste Places

"Awake, awake, Zion, clothe yourself with strength! Put on your garments of splendor… Shake off your dust; rise up, sit enthroned… Free yourself from the chains on your neck."

Isaiah 52:1-2

───*Pause. Take a few deep breaths. Now rest—and abide in Him.*───

Years ago, while I was struggling in my marriage, I did a Bible-marking plan, where I highlighted God's promises in yellow. I chose promises that gave me hope for what I was going through. As a result, I fell in love with the book of Isaiah. In fact, if you opened my Bible to Isaiah today, it's highlighted so often that it looks like a toddler got ahold of a pack of highlighters and went to town!

The book of Isaiah spoke hope into my life when I needed it most. It taught me that my story wasn't over, that I could even dream again, and that God still had a plan for my life. Which, at the time, felt unimaginable. Friend, your life has a great purpose, too.

While the book of Isaiah deals with the failings of the Israelites, it also paints a vivid picture of God's restoration. There's a great richness in those verses.

In Isaiah 43:18-19 it says, "Forget the former things; do not dwell on the past. See, I am doing a new thing! Now it springs up; do you not perceive it? I am making a way in the wilderness and streams in the wasteland." And in Isaiah 58:6-12, God calls us to a life of purpose-filled service, promising that our healing will "spring forth speedily" as we care for the oppressed, the naked, and "loose the bands of wickedness."

But, friend, let's be real for a moment, because we don't always hear this part in our churches: God is not calling us to give from empty wells.

When my family and I served overseas, we saw entire villages that relied on one water well. If that well went dry, it sputtered out only muddy drops, not fit to help anyone. But when the well was full, it provided life-giving water to all who came.

In the same way, God calls us to serve from a place of fullness—not when we're running on empty and back in survival mode. Our wells have to be filled with Him first, because then our service overflows from that place, offering refreshment, hope, and life to those around us.

Beloved, my hope is that you are entering a season of strength and growth—a season where you can reach out a hand to someone walking the path you once traveled, or a different path but still in need of support. You've learned much on your journey and possess wisdom to share—whether a kind word, or insight from your own seasons of pain.

God promises as you "extend your soul to the hungry and satisfy the afflicted soul, then your light shall dawn in the darkness, and your darkness shall be as the noonday" (Isaiah 58:10, NKJV).

Is God calling you today to rise, "shake off your dust... and clothe yourself with strength?" When you're ready, sweet friend,

I believe that He has an important work for you to do—one that flows from a heart that has been filled and restored.

Prayer:

Dear Heavenly Father, help me to see those in need around me. Show me how reaching out to others can be a part of my own healing. Remind me that staying focused only on my own pain for too long can keep me focused inward, and while I need to process my pain to heal, You are always inviting me to grow and to rise higher, step by step, into the fullness of the life You have for me. Amen.

Reflection:

Is there someone on you heart right now that you could encourage, support, or bless in some small way?

–Pause. Take a deep breath. What's one small step in your healing you–
can celebrate today?

Day 84
Letting Go of the Old Narrative

"To appoint unto them that mourn in Zion, to give unto them beauty for ashes, the oil of joy for mourning, the garment of praise for the spirit of heaviness; that they might be called trees of righteousness, the planting of the Lord, that he might be glorified."
Isaiah 61:3, KJV

——*Pause. Take a few deep breaths. Now rest—and abide in Him.*——

The next time you feel "broken" or wish your story had gone differently, remember God is in the business of making beauty for ashes (Isaiah 61:3). And He longs to do this for you, too.

He is not finished writing your story. He can take what feels shattered, painful, or unredeemable and gently weave it into a story filled with hope and purpose.

This is especially true for those who have carried trauma, betrayal, or years of hurt—or for those who mourn, feel silenced, or live under a spirit of heaviness. God sees you. He knows the depth of your pain. And he wants to take the old narratives—the shame, the fear, the story that whispers, *I'm broken beyond repair*—and rewrite them into a love story of redemption. The story of how He is healing you, even now.

Listen to the words God spoke through Isaiah:

> To appoint unto them that mourn in Zion, to give unto them beauty for ashes, the oil of joy for mourning, the garment of praise for the spirit of heaviness; that they might be called trees of righteousness, the planting of the Lord, that he might be glorified (Isaiah 61:3, KJV).

Think of the Japanese artform, *Kintsugi*. It's a centuries-old practice of taking broken pottery pieces and fusing them back together with gold. Each crack becomes a feature of beauty rather than a flaw to hide. The pottery doesn't return to its original shape—it becomes stronger, more beautiful, and uniquely its own. This is how God works with us. He doesn't hide or erase what feels like our broken pieces, our scars, or our past abuse—He redeems them, using each one as part of the masterpiece He is creating.

If you've carried shame, fear, or the story of abuse or betrayal for years, God sees those pieces. He doesn't rush you. He doesn't demand that you "get over it" or "forgive and move on" before you're ready. God is patient.

Jeremiah reminds us that we are like clay in the Father's hands, moldable, redeemable:

> The vessel that He made of clay was marred... so He made it again another vessel, as seemed good to the potter... Behold, as the clay is in the potter's hand, so are you in my hand (Jeremiah 18.4-6).

With the skill of the potter's hands, He shapes and reforms gently, and as He does, our pain slowly turns into purpose. Every scar, tear, and memory become part of a recreated vessel that reflects His glory.

Dear friend, your past does not have to define you. It has simply prepared the soil in which you are planted—for growth, resilience, and a testimony that can comfort and inspire others who are hurting. Like a diamond under pressure, we shine the brightest after our trials. I believe this is because we gain a depth of wisdom we wouldn't have otherwise.

So today, instead of hiding your wounds or feeling ashamed of your struggles, you can take them to God. You can give Him your pain and your doubts. He promises to create something new: a story of courage, hope, and beauty that only He can write.

"My grace is sufficient for thee: for my strength is made perfect in weakness" (2 Corinthians 12:9).

Prayer:

Dear Father, I don't always see the good in my story. Help me to remember that healing takes time and that I don't have to rush what You're still working on. And when I am tired of waiting, please help me to be patient. Teach me to rest in Your hands, trust in Your timing, and to believe that You are writing my story into something good. Amen.

Reflection:

What part of your story still feels too broken to redeem? Ask God to meet you there—with His tenderness.

—Pause. Take a deep breath. What's one small step in your healing you can celebrate today?

Day 85

Rising Higher

"But those who wait on the Lord shall renew their strength; they shall mount up with wings like eagles, they shall run and not be weary, they shall walk and not faint."

Isaiah 40:31, NKJV

———*Pause. Take a few deep breaths. Now rest—and abide in Him.*———

The journey through healing from an unsafe or unsustainable marriage is like climbing a mountain that can feel never-ending. There are days when I cried out to God, "Remove my mountain!" The climb feels too hard.

Maybe you've been there, too—another step in healing or rebuilding life feels like it could push you to exhaustion—yet He gently calls to us: "Keep climbing—we're not there yet."

I want to resist: "But Lord, I'm tired and sore! I don't want to climb anymore." Yet He invites me to take one more step toward restoration: "Come higher, keep moving forward, I'm with you." Along the path, He shows me glimpses of something better at the summit, holding my hand when the path feels jagged and uncertain.

Fear grips me, and I want to stop. Then I realize: If I stop, I risk stagnation. Remaining in the valley of past pain and missed possibilities won't help me move forward. I would miss the amazing things He has planned at the height of my journey toward healing and a renewed life.

This climb is not a call to endure abuse or dysfunction—it's the journey of true healing, of reclaiming your life and identity in Christ. When I struggle, I remind myself of the ultimate climb my Savior took in Gethsemane, just for me. His challenges were the greatest imaginable, and though He prayed for His cup to pass, His Father called Him to continue.

In my hardest moments, I'm reminded that Christ endured so I won't "grow weary or lose heart" (Hebrews 12:3).

At times the Lord may gently discipline us in love or nudge us to examine any hard spots left in our hearts—but never to hurt us. He wants us to flourish without the lingering shadows of past pain. If He calls us to continue climbing on this path of healing, it's toward life, freedom, and hope, not intentional pain.

If you're weary from your journey of healing, turn your eyes to Jesus. The summit is where rest, restoration, and hope await. Our earthly mountains are just steps toward the heights our Savior wants us to reach—far higher than the dark valleys of our past.

Lean in, sweet sister, into the Lord. Allow Him to transform you into His image-bearer and show the world that even jagged mountains can be overcome through the One who has already overcome the world. He believes in you and promises to climb beside you.

Prayer:

Dear Lord, some days I'm tired of climbing. I don't even want to see the view from the top, and I'm tempted to slide back into my old valley. Give me the courage and strength to keep going. Help me to remember the sacrifice You made for me so I can rest my heavy burdens on You as I climb. Help me to rise toward newness and wholeness in You. Amen.

Reflection:

What is one small step you can take today to keep moving forward on your path of healing, trusting that God will carry you when you feel too tired to climb on your own?

—Pause. Take a deep breath. What's one small step in your healing you can celebrate today?

Day 86

God's Justice is Sure

"And I am weak today, though anointed king; and these men, the sons of Zeruiah, are too harsh for me. The Lord shall repay the evildoer according to his wickedness."

2 Samuel 3:39, NKJV

——*Pause. Take a few deep breaths. Now rest—and abide in Him.*——

When you're the target of slander, gossip, or mistreatment, it cuts deeply. We live in a fallen world where the love of many has grown cold (Matthew 24:12), and it hurts to be caught in the crossfire of malicious people.

Even King David, God's anointed, felt weak at times. Second Samuel 3:39 says: "And today, though I am the anointed king, I am weak, and these sons of Zeruiah are too strong for me. May the Lord repay the evildoer according to his evil deeds."

Notice two truths in this verse. First, David acknowledged his weakness but reaffirmed his identity: He *was* anointed. No amount of slander or false accusations can change the fact that you are God's child, a "royal priesthood—a chosen generation"

(1 Peter 2:9). Your worth is not determined by the words of others but by God's love for you.

Second, God promises justice. The Lord will reward the doer of evil according to his wickedness. You don't have to carry this burden or feel compelled to retaliate—God will fight your battles (Exodus 14:13-14). Stand still and see the salvation of the Lord. Standing still doesn't mean we ignore practical wisdom or safety measures, but we don't have to carry the burden of vengeance ourselves.

David's honesty shows us it's OK to feel overwhelmed. It's OK if today feels heavy or your heart is hurting. You don't always have to be strong—God sees you just as you are and is with you. Being chosen by God does not mean we won't have hard days, encounter difficult people, or face enemies. But our circumstances don't change who we are in Him.

Take courage, because when you're weak, God is strong (2 Corinthians 12:9-10). No matter how cutting the words or actions of others, you are still fearfully and wonderfully made—the apple of His eye (Psalm 139:14, Psalm 17:8).

You may feel weak today, but your God is bigger, and you are still His chosen. Trust Him to vindicate you in His timing, because He promises He will reward each person according to their deeds. Your peace is found in Him, and your identity is secure.

Prayer:

Dear God, please help me to rest my case in Your hands. Help me to know You will deal with those who trouble me. I don't have to. Thank You for being my defender and protector. Amen.

Reflection:

What words or actions from others have left you feeling weak, hurt, or unsettled? How do you want to respond? How can you remind yourself that you don't have to carry the burden of retaliation or approval from others?

*–Pause. Take a deep breath. What's one small step in your healing you–
can celebrate today?*

Day 87

Sorrow and Joy Mingled

"Lord, I believe; help my unbelief!"
Mark 9:24

——*Pause. Take a few deep breaths. Now rest—and abide in Him.*——

I saw a photo one day that said: Grief and Gratitude can exist simultaneously. Hope and Heartache can live in the same space. Joy and Sorrow can both be present (credit: Grace Filled Growth).

This resonated deeply with me. It echoes what many of us have lived. Maybe you, too, have experienced this dichotomy. There will be dark times, and when they come, they can feel like a thundering wave crashing down around us. I know it's not easy, I've been there—more times that I can count, and it's tough.

These are the things that nobody wishes to go through. But it's during these seasons of seemingly unending pain where our fortitude is built, our resiliency is gaining a foundation, and our ability to see hope even in the darkness is being developed. And no, *these are not* easy experiences. In fact, they're some of the hardest and most painful we'll ever go through.

But if we let them, these seasons can shape us in ways we don't yet see, even if right now they only feel unbearable.

These are the times that teach us the words to say to the next weary traveler that's being swept off their path by their own trials and obstacles. These are the times that can speak into our hearts the deep lessons learned while our Savior lived and walked the same path we're on now.

Scripture says He was a man acquainted with sorrows just as we are (Isaiah 53:3). Christ knows every dark corner, understands every tear we shed, and has experienced every "crashing blow" that could ever come our way. And while that may not be a comfort in your hard season, the real comfort is that while here in this world though we "will have trials and tribulations," in the next life, we will never have another moment of pain nor one tear shed (John 16:33, Revelation 7:17).

Though our trials are not always removed, God promises to walk with us in them. He is patient in our sorrow and grief—and can even help us to mingle joy in the midst of suffering.

I know it's difficult, dear soul, but if we choose Him, even here, amid our trials, God promises that we can have joy despite our pain, even if it comes slowly or feels fragile (James 1:2-4, 1 Peter 1:6-9).

2 Corinthians 6:10 says that as believers we can be: "…sorrowful yet always rejoicing; poor, yet making many rich; having nothing, and yet possessing everything." I understand if this doesn't feel true in the moment of your pain, because sometimes it feels like sorrow is all there is. Yet, God gently invites us to believe that sorrow and joy can live side by side.

I know, I can hear what someone is saying right now… "not today, not now, not in the middle of my deepest hurt and pain—this feels impossible." Friend, I have come to trust that when God says something is possible, it can be—even if it feels impossible today. I don't say that lightly, because I've wrestled with it myself.

I've had those dark seasons when I all but lost my faith wondering if God heard my pleas for help—but He held me tight and didn't release His grip, even when mine felt it would certainly fail. He is that faithful—and He will be for you too.

It is possible for grief and gratitude to exist together, for sorrow and joy to somehow flow from the same heart, and for a victim of this world's wrong to become a victor, who inherits the world to come, and even God's abundance in *this life*.

Prayer:

Dear God, I want to trust You that have seen my pain and will give me joy amid my suffering. I believe, Lord, help my unbelief. I thank You even now for Your answer to my prayer. I praise You for the ways in which You want to reveal Your answers to me, and I praise You for knowing the end from the beginning and this includes my needs and requests. I simply praise You. Amen.

Reflection:

Reflect on where you are with God right now. Even during hurt, doubt, confusion, or healing, can you trust that His goodness endures, and that He can hold your questions and your pain?

–Pause. Take a deep breath. What's one small step in your healing you can celebrate today?

Day 88
The Path of Forgiveness

"If we confess our sins, he is faithful and just to forgive us our sins and to cleanse us from all unrighteousness."
1 John 1:9

——Pause. Take a few deep breaths. Now rest—and abide in Him.——

When someone hurts us deeply, forgiveness can feel impossible. I've been there. But holding onto unforgiveness can be just as heavy. It can turn into bitterness and resentment that spreads like a quiet poison through our hearts, touching everything around us.

Forgiving someone doesn't mean you condone, excuse, or forget their behavior. It's quite the opposite—it's naming the harm for what it was and saying, "I won't allow it to keep hurting me." Forgiveness restores your agency and lets *you* decide how you'll heal. They don't get to have that hold over you any longer.

Some have said, "Jesus let Judas be His disciple; shouldn't we continue to forgive everyone and extend the same grace?" Following Jesus' example doesn't necessarily mean we will do everything He did—He is the Son of God, we're not. He raised the dead; we cannot. His life is the example we're to follow by principle, not always exact replication.

In Judas' case, Jesus knew he would betray him, because it was a prophetic fulfillment. But Jesus didn't shy away from calling out Judas' wrong and giving him an opportunity to repent (Matthew 26:23, Luke 22:48, John 17:12, Luke 22:21). In the end, it was Judas who chose not to.

We're called to, "Be kind to one another, tenderhearted, forgiving one another, *as God in Christ forgave you*" (Ephesians 4:32, emphasis added). But Scripture also says, "If we confess our sins, He is faithful and just to forgive us our sins and to cleanse us from all unrighteousness" (1 John 1:9). Forgiving as Christ forgave doesn't mean it's an exact replication, because clearly, we can't cleanse the sins of others, we're not God. *Our responsibility is to forgive, not to save or enable.*

Forgiveness doesn't mean you have to reconcile or reconnect with an unrepentant person. Sometimes reconnecting isn't safe, and in those cases, forgiveness is something you work through privately with God. He cares about your emotional and physical safety and would not ask you to stay in harm's way.

Yes, God calls us to forgive, because it's the doorway to true freedom. It loosens the grip that pain, hurt, and even trauma can have on us. Over time, it *may* help to disconnect us from the person who caused us harm—by no longer needing to replay the story or feel the old surge of emotions when thinking of them.

Yet many women I've walked alongside wonder if they've truly forgiven because they still feel anger—or find themselves triggered by memories. I believe this is normal.

Forgiveness is a process and a decision of the heart. Our bodies and minds may take longer to heal and come alongside our decision. Sometimes the emotions return, not because we've failed to forgive, but because our nervous system is still processing the pain. God understands and walks with you patiently as this process unfolds.

Forgiveness doesn't happen overnight—the hardest things rarely do. But in time, with His help, it can become a gift of freedom—a release from the weight that was never yours to carry.

And if you're reading this and feel triggered or angry at the thought that a loving God would ask you to forgive someone who has hurt you so deeply, that's understandable. Sometimes the pain is just too raw. It's OK to be where you are.

Take time to process the anger, to grieve your losses, and to let God meet you in the middle of it all. You may even need to forgive yourself. He won't rush or shame you. He waits with us, patiently and tenderly. His gift of peace is ready when you are.

Prayer:

Dear Heavenly Father, I don't know if I'm ready to forgive yet. Please continue to guide me in my healing and, in Your timing, grant me the gift of forgiveness for those who have harmed me. Amen.

Reflection:

Take a moment and think about those who have hurt you. Write down their names, and if you feel ready, ask God to help you forgive. Let Him hold you in this process—it's not always easy, but in the end, it's freeing.

–Pause. Take a deep breath. What's one small step in your healing you can celebrate today?

Day 89

Stacking Stones of Faith

"Do not forget the things your eyes have seen or let them fade from your heart as long as you live. Teach them to your children and to their children after them."

Deuteronomy 4:9

——*Pause. Take a few deep breaths. Now rest—and abide in Him.*——

Years ago, when my family lived in the desert, my son and I loved to hike along the mesas near our home. We often came across neatly stacked piles of rocks called cairns. They were markers placed there to signify a turn or an important spot to help guide hikers, so they wouldn't lose their way.

I can remember my son and I talking about how we imagined they looked like the altars Abraham or other great men of faith in the Bible built on their journey. Altars they erected as memorials that marked God's promises, His presence, and His provisions—or to give thanks and to worship God.

The cairns came to mind one day as I was thinking of my own twists and turns in life. What if we did the same on our journey? What if we paused to mark the places where God met us in our pain, carried us through what seemed impossible, or gave us the courage to take the next step forward?

Each of our lives bears the markings of His faithfulness, just like those who have gone before us. Our healing journeys will look different but the path taken carries deep significance: The moment our fear was surrendered so we could move forward. The moments in which God turned our pain into purpose. The moment we chose a healthier way instead of slipping back into an old pattern. Or the moment we spoke our truth for the first time, despite a trembling voice.

Each of these things is a sacred way marker on our journey that reminds us we have never walked this path alone. I bet if we could see them from heaven's perspective, they would form a beautifully laid out path. The parts of our story that felt crooked and confusing to us, smoothed out by God. As He took the pain that the enemy had for us and turned it into a plan for our healing and growth.

Dear friend, the journey ahead may still be rocky at times. Healing is rarely a straight path. There will be long stretches that feel exhausting, dark valleys that seem endless and wide, and peaks you never thought you could scale. Marking your milestones, *your* cairns, can help remind you of just how far you've come and provide you hope for the future.

As you continue on your journey, don't rush past what God is doing in you and what He has already done for you. Pause to take in His faithfulness. Mark your milestones. Maybe it's as simple as jotting down a note in your journal or whispering a prayer of thanks. Whatever it looks like for you, don't forget to celebrate, even your small steps.

Your story is not just about where you've been, but about the One who has been walking ahead of you all along, guiding you to freedom. Every marker is a testimony. Keep going, dear one. Keep stacking your stones. And as you look back, I pray that instead of seeing a path of brokenness, you'll see a path of grace, marked by the hand of God, who never left your side.

Prayer:

Dear Father, thank You for walking faithfully beside me on my journey. Please help me to mark my victories, even the small ones, and to trust that You will keep guiding me to the very end. Amen.

Reflection:

What have been some of the cairns along your path to healing—the markers that remind you of where God has met you? How can you continue to mark them moving forward, so you can look back and remember His faithfulness on your journey?

–Pause. Take a deep breath. What's one small step in your healing you can celebrate today?

Day 90
Your Crown of Hope

"Although the threads of my life have often seemed knotted, I know, by faith, that on the other side of the embroidery...There is a Crown." Corrie Ten Boom

———*Pause. Take a few deep breaths. Now rest—and abide in Him.*———

Corrie Ten Boom used to carry a small piece of embroidery with her whenever she spoke to large crowds. On one side, the cloth looked like a tangled mess—dark and light threads knotted and crisscrossed, colors running every which way.

"This," she would say, "is how life looks from our side. But God sees the other side."

Then she would turn it over to reveal a beautiful golden crown, adorned with multi-colored jewels—carefully stitched together with those same dark threads.

Corrie understood pain. She had lost most of her family in the concentration camps of World War II. She had seen evil up close and yet stood before crowds holding out that piece of cloth—a quiet testimony that suffering, somehow, was not wasted in the hands of God.

Our lives can look like that, too—tangled and confusing, the dark threads representing our hardest seasons, seemingly impossible to make sense of. We look down at the mess and wonder if anything good could ever come from it. *But God sees the crown.* He has not finished weaving yet.

Maybe you've walked through devastation—abuse, betrayal, deep loss. Maybe it's taken every ounce of strength just to keep standing. You've fought hard for healing, and maybe you're still fighting. And still, the threads don't make sense.

Sweet friend, I know how exhausting that can be. But please know—God is still at work on the other side of the cloth.

Years ago, I heard a young pastor, filled with wisdom beyond his years, say: "Time is the canvas on which God paints, and eternity is the perspective from which we will see the beauty of His handiwork." — Daniel Venegas

When you can't see the beauty yet—when the pain still feels bigger than the purpose—trust that eternity will tell the rest of the story.

I remember in some of the darkest seasons of my own life, when I couldn't fathom how the broken pieces could ever serve a purpose, my mother used to say, "Darah, you may not see it now, but I just know God will use these experiences for something good in your future."

And now, I'm here to say the same to you: He will use your pain for good—all of it.

Every broken moment that once whispered "lost" can one day testify "redeemed." Every scar that once felt like proof of your pain can become evidence of His healing. But you have to let Him keep weaving.

Healing doesn't happen overnight. It's a slow, sacred work. Even as you heal, God is weaving your story into something eternal—a crown of beauty where there were once ashes, strength where there was once only survival.

Jeremiah 29:11 isn't a promise that life will be easy—context shows us otherwise. It's a reminder that God's plans are filled with hope, even when our struggle continues. God can take the chains of our captivity and turn them into the threads of our freedom.

And He can transform pain into purpose, and our wilderness journey into our testimony.

You have walked through the fire, but you're still here. And that, friend, is no small thing. God hasn't wasted a single thread.

When all is said and done—when we stand on the other side of eternity and finally see what He was creating all along—we'll understand.

It was never just broken pieces and dark seasons.

It was the making of a crown.

Prayer:

Dear Lord, as I go forward, help me to remember that hope is not found in the absence of trials, but in You. Help me to hold my head high and wear my crown well. Help me to follow You all the days of my life, and trust that You are truly, not tritely, working all things for my ultimate good. Fill me with courage, dignity, strength, and inner peace as I continue toward the beautiful future You have waiting for me. Amen.

Reflection:

Write down your vision for the future. What does moving forward look like? You don't have to tackle your plans all at once, just one step at a time. And as you do, God promises to weave even your hardest moments into something beautiful—as you now emerge stronger and rise higher.

You've got this, sweet friend. Pause, take a deep breath, and step into the future God has waiting for you as you spread your wings and fly free.

Additional Resources:

The following resources are available to help you continue growing and healing.

Each resource is to help support your ongoing journey toward clarity, safety, and wholeness.

You can download or access all materials at:

www.darahashlie.com/rewrittenandrising

- Printable Safety Plan
- Emotional Abuse Questionairre
- Support Groups and Courses for Survivors
- Support Groups for Abusive Spouses
- Signs of True Change Handout
- Dating Again – Red Flags & Green Flags
- Helping Children Navigate Harm in the Home
- When God Seems to Bless an Abuser's Ministry
- How to Navigate Repeating Arguments/Boundaries
- Pornography Blocking Sites and Recommended Resources
- Why Couples Counseling is Not Helpful For Some Marriages

D.A.N.G.E.R. CHECK

How to Assess for Safety

D – Domination & Deadly Threats

- Has your partner threatened to kill you, themselves, or others?
- Does he control you or say things like, *"If I can't have you, no one can"*?
- Has he ever used or shown weapons, or choked/strangled you?
- Has he abused you when pregnant?
- Has he ever forced you to have sex?
- Has he been violent toward you or anyone else before?

These are top homicide risk factors. Don't wait for "proof." Get help now.

A – Access to Weapons & Abuse Escalation

- Are there guns, knives, or other weapons in the home?
- Has his anger or violence increased—more frequent, intense, or unpredictable?

Access to weapons and escalation can both lead to extreme danger.

N – Narcissistic Tendencies & Isolation/Control

- Does he dehumanize you, lack empathy, or show little regard for your feelings or life?
- Is he charming in public but a different person in private? Like a Dr. Jekyll and Mr. Hyde persona.
- Does he believe he "owns" you, monitors your phone, limits friends, or controls your money?

A "double life," a secret life, or an ownership mindset can increase your danger risk.

G – Growing Mental Instability or History of Mental Illness

- Has he shown signs of depression, paranoia, or hopelessness ("There's no point in living")?
- Does he make suicidal or homicidal threats?
- Has he stopped taking medication or refused help for serious mental illness?
- Is there a history of mental illness in his family?

Emotional instability can escalate to lethal decisions.

E – Excessive Jealousy & Entitlement

- Are you constantly accused of cheating or flirting?
- Has there been stalking or restraining orders?
- Does he explode when you seek independence or connection with others?

Separation or perceived rejection can trigger dangerous reactions.

R – Reckless Behavior *and/or* Alcohol & Drug Use

- Does he frequently abuse alcohol or drugs? While substance use doesn't cause abuse, it can lower inhibitions and lead to increased danger when abuse is present.
- Does he drive recklessly, hurt animals, or threaten your children or family?
- Does he submit to authority or is he rebellious toward authority figures? Does he have people who hold him accountable?

Substance misuse, recklessness, disregard of authority, or harm to pets or others increase the risks for danger.

It's important to note that the most dangerous time in an abusive relationship is when the victim tries to leave. Even if there has not been previous physical violence, this can still be a dangerous time. Abuse often escalates when an abusive person starts to lose control over their victim. If you ever feel unsafe, don't wait, reach out for help.

You can contact the National Domestic Violence Hotline (U.S.) at 800.799.SAFE (7233) or visit: thehotline.org, or contact your local domestic violence shelter.

If you believe you are in immediate danger, call 911 right away.

Note: this is an awareness guide, not a formal danger assessment.[1,2]

About the Author

Darah Ashlie is an author, speaker, and President and Founder of Restore and Rise Ministries. She holds a master's degree in counseling and works with women as a Christian coach in her private practice. She runs programs for women to help them rebuild and recover after trauma and abuse and leads trainings to help equip churches to wisely protect the vulnerable and respond with compassion to survivors of intimate partner violence and abuse.

Ongoing Support for Survivors:

If you're a woman looking to continue your journey of restoration, Restore and Rise Ministries offers:

- Private coaching, courses, and resources
- A safe, faith-centered community for healing

Continue your journey here: www.restoreandriseministries.org

Speaking and Training:

Darah Ashlie is available to speak and conduct trainings at conferences, women's ministries, and church events, bringing a voice that is both steady and soulful, offering hope, insight, and practical guidance for navigating abuse and restoration. Her messages and trainings offer a rare blend of survivor wisdom and trauma-informed insights. She offers practical guidance on:

- Responding to domestic violence and abuse
- Protecting the vulnerable in your congregation or ministry
- Navigating trauma and faith with compassion and wisdom

For more information on speaking or trainings:
www.darahashlie.com/called-to-protect

Notes

Foundations for Your Journey

1. Gottman, John, and Nan Silver. *The Seven Principles for Making Marriage Work*. London: Orion Spring, 2023
2. Holmes, Stephanie C., Dan Holmes, Sydney Holmes, and Erica Holmes. Embracing the autism spectrum: *Finding Hope & Joy Navigating the Neurodiverse Family Journey*. United States: Autism Spectrum Resources for Marriage and Family, LLC, 2023.
3. Vernick, Leslie. *The Emotionally Destructive Marriage: How to Find Your Voice and Reclaim Your Hope*. CO Springs, CO: WaterBrook Press, 2013

Day 33: The Lies that Keep Us Stuck

1. List partially adapted from: Blythe, Anne. "10 Lies That Keep Women Stuck." Instagram, September 29, 2025. https://www.instagram.com/reel/DPMAJTNkb_2/.

Day 41: Navigating Triggers, When the Past Finds You

1. Colbert, Don. *Deadly Emotions: Understand the Mind-Body-Spirit Connection That Can Heal or Destroy You*. Nashville, TN: Thomas Nelson, 2020.
2. Eriksson, Cynthia. "Thriving Through Trauma: Five R's for Resilience and Recovery." Thrive Center, September 7, 2024. https://thethrivecenter.org/thriving-through-trauma-the-5-rs-of-resilience-and-recovery/.

Day 61: Choosing the Good Despite the Hard

1. Emmons, R. A., & McCullough, M. E. (2003). *Counting Blessings Versus Burdens: An Experimental Investigation of Gratitude and Subjective Well-being in Daily Life*. Journal of Personality and Social Psychology, 84(2), 377–389.
2. Wood, A. M., Froh, J. J., & Geraghty, A. W. A. (2010). *Gratitude and Well-being: A Review and Theoretical Integration. Clinical Psychology Review, 30(7), 890–905*.

Day 69: Who Can You Trust, Identifying Safe People

1. List partially based on research from: Brown, Brené. *Braving the Wilderness: The quest for True Belonging and the Courage to Stand Alone*. New York: Random House, 2019.

Danger Assessment

1. Campbell, Jacquelyn C, Daniel W Webster, and Nancy Glass. "The Danger Assessment: Validation of a Lethality Risk Assessment Instrument for Intimate Partner Femicide." Journal of interpersonal violence, April 2009. https://pmc.ncbi.nlm.nih.gov/articles/PMC7878014/.
2. Vernick, Leslie. Signs of Danger Mean Time to Flee, August 23, 2017. https://leslievernick.com/blog/signs-danger-mean-time-flee/.

www.ingramcontent.com/pod-product-compliance
Lightning Source LLC
Chambersburg PA
CBHW071206090426
42736CB00014B/2732